Insight

Important Sociological Issues in the 21st Century

Roy V. Lewis, Ph.D.

Other Books by Roy V. Lewis

Nonfiction

Juvenile Diversion (With Dr. Ted Palmer), 1980

White Collar Crime and Offenders: A 20-Year Longitudinal Cohort Study, 2002

Trouble in Paradise: The Decline of Christianity in the 21st Century, 2009

The Reasoned Society [Rational Critique on Issues of the Day] Series I, 2009

The Reasoned Society [Rational Critique on Issues of the Day] Series II, 2010

Insight: Sociology and Critique of Today's Cultural Issues, 2013

Insight: Critical Social Issues of Our Time, 2013

Sociology of Today's Social Issues, 2015

Lurking in the Shadows, 2015

Fiction

American Hawk, 2003

Night of the Cougar, 2007

Jackals' Lair, 2010

Insight

Important Sociological Issues in the 21st Century

Table of Contents

Politics

Chapter 1 President Obama's Real
Accomplishments in Office

Chapter 2 Tea Party in America, Lunatic
Fringe or New Face of the
Republican Party

Chapter 3 The 2014 Midterm Elections: The
Future of the Republican Party in
America

Chapter 4 The Arrogance of Power, the Vile
History of the CIA

Chapter 5 Destruction of the Universal
Declaration of Human Rights by
the CIA

Fitness/Exercise

Chapter 6 2015: Losing Weight and Getting Into Shape in the New Year [a Two-Part Series], Part I

Chapter 7 2015: Losing Weight and Getting Into Shape in the New Year [a Two-Part Series], Part II

Chapter 8 The Coming Revolution in Bodybuilding---Maximum Contraction Training [The Science Behind How Muscles Get Larger]

Religion

Chapter 9 The Truth Value of the Holy Bible

Psychology

Chapter 10 The Mind Brain/Mind Body
Dichotomy

Chapter 11 A New Social Psychology
Theory of Human Need
Fulfillment

About the Author

Politics

Chapter 1

President Obama's Real Accomplishments in Office

Introduction

Where politics is concerned there always seems to be a real disconnect between facts on the one hand, and political rhetoric espoused by the media and the various political parties on the other. Citizens expect the media to decipher fact from fiction. But since the media is often biased in favor of one political party over another, the voting public is actually left to their own devices to determine fact from fiction.

As a consequence, the average citizen is left out in the cold where unbiased evaluation of a candidate for political office is concerned. As we all know, politicians talk more about values, not facts. Facts are often used to measure results of a politician's programs, while values are used to make promises and to encourage the public to vote for a particular candidate. Facts are too dangerous for politicians while values are safer when interacting with the public.

Purpose of Chapter

The purpose of this chapter is to present to the public a factual review of the real accomplishments of the President of the United States, Barack Obama. I will review his accomplishments in two ways: Review the two most important promises the President made back in 2008 which were to lower the unemployment rate and create middle class jobs for Americans. The second way is to list the accomplishments of Barack Obama.

When it came to the President's promises in 2008, both related to economics. This was important since the country came close to a financial disaster and collapse during President Bush's last term in office.

At the time he made his promises, little did he know that his vision for America would be met by a recalcitrant and often times obstreperous Congress, particularly the House of Representatives. Despite the juggernaut of destructive gridlock offered up by the Republican Party and its Tea Party members, achievements were made in the last 7 years by the President.

The Promises of President Obama

The first promise was to lower the unemployment rate, and the second was to create jobs for middle-class Americans. I will present data that supports these promises, and I will carefully review actual achievements.

The Unemployment Rate

The President took office in January 2009. At that time the unemployment rate had been climbing during the previous year under the Bush Administration from 5.0 percent in January 2008 to 7.8 percent in January, 2009.

The rate of unemployment continued to rise to a high of 10 percent in October 2009 as a lagging effect of the recession and near financial collapse in 2008. It continued to drift from 9.9 down to 9.4 percent during the rest of 2009, and continued through to the end of 2010.

By this time the policies of the President and the Federal Reserve Board (primarily the economic stimulus packages) were starting to have an effect on the unemployment rate. In January 2011 the unemployment rate dropped to 9.1 percent.

A year later it was 8.2 percent. By January 2013 it was 7.9 percent. In January 2014 the unemployment rate had dropped to 6.6 percent. In June 2014 the unemployment rate dropped again to 6.1 percent. During the President's watch, the unemployment rate declined 39 percent. As of August 2014 the unemployment rate still stayed at 6.1 percent. However, by April, 2015 the unemployment rate was a fantastic 5.4%.

It would, of course, be simplistic and rather naïve to either ascribe total credit or total blame to the person holding office of the presidency for the lion's share of any economic change. The reality is economic cycles and the economy itself, each have a life of its own. Nevertheless, fiscal and economic policies of any President do matter. So from a policy standpoint, President Barack Obama has very much helped impact the unemployment rate in a positive way, thus achieving his first promise. It went from a high of 10% in

October, 2009 to a low of 5.4% in April, 2o15.

Job Creation and Growth

It is a fact that, since President Roosevelt, the average amount of private sector jobs created during Democratic Presidential terms is 1,463,220 and the average amount during Republican Presidential terms is a paltry 642,000 jobs.

Obama's Second Promise

52 Straight Months of Private Sector Job Growth

July 3, 2014

Under President Obama's leadership, the economy has added private sector jobs for 52 straight months. During this span, 9.7

million private sector jobs have been created. In the Senate, Democrats are fighting to continue this positive trend and help speed along the economic recovery.

President Obama's Major Accomplishments

What follows is a PARTIAL list of Obama's accomplishments so far.

Despite the characterizations of some Republicans, Obama's success rate in winning congressional votes on issues was an unprecedented 96.7% for his first year in office. Though he is often cited as superior to Obama, President Lyndon Johnson's success rate in 1965 was only 93%.

Fiscal Responsibility

Within days after taking office, Obama signed an Executive Order ordering an audit of government contracts, and combating waste and abuse. The President created the post of Chief Performance Officer, whose job it is to make operations more efficient to save the federal government money. On his first full day, he froze White House salaries.

He appointed the first Federal Chief Information Officer to oversee federal IT spending. He committed to phasing out unnecessary and outdated weapons systems, and also signed the Weapons Systems Acquisition Reform Act to stop waste, fraud and abuse in the defense procurement and contracting system. Through an executive order, he created the National Commission on Fiscal Responsibility and Reform.

Improving the Economy, Preventing Depression

Obama pushed through and signed the American Recovery and Reinvestment Act, otherwise known as "the stimulus package," despite the fact that not one Republican voted for that bill. In addition, he launched recovery.gov, so that taxpayers could track spending from the Act.

In his first year, the American Recovery and Reinvestment Act created and sustained 2.1 million jobs and stimulated the economy 3.5%. Obama completed the massive TARP financial and banking rescue plan, and recovered virtually all of its costs. He created the Making Home Affordable home refinancing plan.

Obama oversaw the creation of more jobs in 2010 alone than Bush did in eight years. He oversaw a bailout of General Motors that saved at least 1.4 million jobs, and put pressure on the company to change its practices, resulting in GM returning to its place as the top car company in the world.

Obama also doubled funding for the Manufacturing Extension Partnership which is designed to improve manufacturing efficiency.

He signed the Fraud Enforcement and Recovery Act giving the federal government more tools to investigate and prosecute fraud in every corner of the financial system. It also created a bipartisan Financial Crisis Inquiry Commission to investigate the financial fraud that led to the economic meltdown.

Obama signed the Credit Card Accountability, Responsibility and Disclosure (CARD) Act, which was designed to protect consumers from unfair and deceptive credit card practices. He increased infrastructure spending after years of neglect. Obama signed the Helping Families Save Their Homes Act, expanding on the Making Home Affordable Program to help millions of Americans avoid preventable foreclosures. The bill also provided $2.2 billion to help combat homelessness, and to stabilize the housing market.

Through the Worker, Home Ownership, and Business Assistance Act of 2009, Obama and Congressional Democrats provided tax credits to first-time home buyers, which helped the U.S. housing market recovery. He initiated a $15 billion plan designed to encourage increased lending to small businesses.

Obama created business.gov, which allows for online collaboration between small businesses and experts re-managing a business. (The program has since merged with SBA.gov.) He played a lead role in getting the G-20 Summit to commit to a $1.1 trillion deal to combat the global financial crisis. Obama took steps to improve minority access to capital. He created a $60 billion bank to fund infrastructure improvements such as roads and bridges.

He implemented an auto industry rescue plan, and saved as many as 1 million jobs. Many are of the opinion that he saved the entire auto industry, and even the economy of the entire Midwest. Through the American Recovery and Reinvestment Act, Obama saved at least 300,000 education jobs, such as teachers, principals, librarians, and counselors that would have otherwise been lost. Obama dismantled the Minerals Management Service, thereby moving forward to cut ties between energy companies and the government.

He provided funding to states and the Department of Homeland Security to save thousands of police and firefighter jobs from being cut during the recession.

He used recovered TARP money to fund programs at local housing finance agencies in California, Florida, Nevada, Arizona and Michigan. Obama crafted an Executive order establishing the President's Advisory Council on Financial Capability to assist in financial education for all Americans.

Wall Street Reforms and Consumer Protection

Obama ordered 65 executives who took bailout money to cut their own pay until they paid back all bailout money.

He pushed through and got passed Dodd-Frank, one of the largest and most comprehensive Wall Street reforms since the Great Depression. Dodd-Frank also included the creation of the Consumer Financial Protection Bureau. Obama made it so that banks could no longer use YOUR money to invest in high-risk financial instruments that work against their own customers' interests.

He supported the concept of allowing stockholders to vote on executive compensation. Obama wholly endorsed and supported the Foreign Account Tax Compliance Act of 2009 that would close offshore tax avoidance loopholes. He made a deal with Swiss banks that permit the US government to gain access to the records of criminals and tax evaders. He established a Consumer Protection Financial Bureau designed to protect consumers from financial sector excesses.

Obama oversaw and then signed the most sweeping food safety legislation since the Great Depression.

Civil Rights and Anti-Discrimination

Obama advocated for and signed the Matthew Shepard and James Byrd, Jr. Hate Crimes Prevention Act, which made it a federal crime to assault anyone based on his or her sexual orientation or gender identity.

He pushed through, signed and demanded the Pentagon enact a repeal of the discriminatory "Don't Ask Don't Tell" policy that forced soldiers to lie to fight for their country, and put our troops at risk by disqualifying many qualified soldiers from helping. Obama appointed Kareem Dale as the first ever Special Assistant to the President for Disability Policy. Helped Congress pass and signed the Civil Rights History Act. He extended benefits to same-sex partners of federal employees.

Obama has appointed more openly gay officials than anyone in history. He issued a Presidential Memorandum reaffirming the rights of gay couples to make medical decisions for each other. He established a White House Council on Women and Girls.

He signed the Lilly Ledbetter Fair Pay Act, restoring basic protections against pay discrimination for women and other workers. This was after the GOP blocked the bill in 2007. Only 5 Republican Senators voted for the bill.

Obama wrote and signed an Executive Order establishing a White House Council on Women and Girls to ensure that all Cabinet and Cabinet-level agencies evaluate the effect of their policies and programs on women and families.

He expanded funding for the Violence against Women Act.

Under Obama's watch, National Labor Relations Board has issued final rules that require all employers to prominently post employees' rights where all employees or prospective employees can see it, including websites and intranets, beginning November 2011.

Fighting Poverty

Obama provided a $20 billion increase for the Supplemental Nutrition Assistance Program (Food Stamps). He signed an Executive Order that established the White House Office of Urban Affairs.

Improved Foreign Relations and American Status Abroad

Obama visited more countries and met with more world leaders than any previous president during his first six months in office.

As he promised, he gave a speech at a major Islamic forum in Cairo early in his administration.

He did much to restore America's reputation around the world as a global leader that does the "right thing" in world affairs, at least according to the rest of the planet.

He re-established and reinforced our partnership with NATO and other allies on strategic international issues.

Closed a number of secret detention facilities.

Obama improved relations with Middle East countries by appointing special envoys.

He pushed for military to emphasize development of foreign language skills.

Offered $400 million to the people living in Gaza, called on both Israel and the Palestinians to stop inciting violence. He refused to give Israel the green light to attack Iran over their possible nuclear program. He worked to make donations to Haiti tax-deductible in 2009. He established a new U.S.-China Strategic and Economic Dialogue.

Issued an Executive Order blocking interference with and helped to stabilize Somalia.

He established new, more reasonable policies in our relations with Cuba, such as allowing Cuban-Americans to visit their families and send money to support them. Since then he has opened up relations with Cuba altogether.

He ordered the closure of the prison at Guantanamo Bay. It was Republicans (and a smattering of Democrats) who prevented him from following through.

Obama ordered a review of our detention and interrogation policy, and prohibited the use of torture, or what Bush called "enhanced interrogation." He ordered interrogators to limit their actions to the Army Field manual. He ordered all secret detention facilities in Eastern Europe and elsewhere to be closed. **He released the Bush torture memos.**

On his second day in office, he signed a detailed Executive Order that banned torture, reversed all Bush torture policies, and put the United States in compliance with the Geneva Convention. However, when the Senate Report on Torture of prisoners was released in 2014, he did not hold accountable those who had committed crimes against humanity.

In response to the emerging "Arab Spring," he created a Rapid Response fund, to assist emerging democracies with foreign aid, debt relief, and technical assistance and investment packages in order to show that the United States stands with them.

Obama passed the Iran Sanctions Act, to prevent war, and to encourage Iran to give up their nuclear program. Obama ended the

Iraq War. In response to current events with an ISIS invasion in Iraq, President Obama ordered air strikes and offered humanitarian assistance to Iraq religious minorities under threat of death from ISIS. He has now created an international coalition through NATO to annihilate ISIS in Iraq and Syria.

He authorized and oversaw a secret mission by SEAL Team Six to rescue two hostages held by Somali pirates. The importance of this international act of terrorism was later made into a movie with Tom Hanks.

Better Approach to Defense

Obama created a comprehensive new strategy for dealing with the international nuclear threat. He authorized a $1.4 billion reduction in Star Wars program in 2010. He restarted nuclear nonproliferation talks and built up the nuclear inspection infrastructure/protocols to where they had been before Bush.

He signed and pushed to ratification a new SALT Treaty.

He also negotiated and signed a new START Treaty that will last until at least 2021. Through the Defense Authorization Act, he reversed the Bush Administration and committed to no permanent military bases in Iraq.

He developed the first comprehensive strategy with regard to Afghanistan and Pakistan designed to facilitate the defeat of al Qaeda and the withdrawal of most troops, as well as the rebuilding of Afghanistan. He returned our focus to Afghanistan, stabilized the country, and began the process of withdrawing our troops.

Obama fulfilled his campaign promise and ended our involvement in Iraq in 2011. However, current events have altered a total and complete withdrawal from Iraq. Despite the current problems in Iraq the president, during his administration, has taken steps to severely weaken al Qaeda and limit their ability to terrorize the world. Many of the top al Qaeda leaders have been killed or otherwise neutralized.

He negotiated and signed a nuclear nonproliferation treaty with India.

He took decisive action to use NATO to limit the slaughter of innocents in Libya, so that the Libyan people could topple a despotic government and determine their own fate.

Veterans

He made sure that families of fallen soldiers could be on hand when the body arrives at Dover AFB by providing funding for it. He also ended the media blackout on coverage of the return of fallen soldiers.

He funded Department of Veterans Affairs (VA) with an extra $1.4 billion to improve veterans' services.

He provided the troops with better body armor. He created the Joint Virtual Lifetime Electronic Record program for military personnel in order to improve the quality of their medical care.

He put an end to the Bush-era stop-loss policy that kept soldiers in Iraq/Afghanistan beyond their enlistment date.

He supported and signed the Veterans Health Care Budget Reform and Transparency Act, which made more money available to enable better medical care for veterans.

He ushered through the largest spending increase in 30 years for the Department of Veterans Affairs for improved medical facilities, and to assist states in acquiring or constructing state nursing homes and extended care facilities.

He created the Green Vet Initiative, which provided special funding to the Labor Department to provide veterans with training in green jobs.

He oversaw a $4.6 billion expansion of the Veterans Administration budget to pay for more mental health professionals.

Education

He has repeatedly increased funding for student financial aid and, at the same time, cut the banks completely out of the process.

He completely reformed the student loan program to make it possible for students to refinance at a lower rate.

Through the American Recovery and Reinvestment Act, he invested heavily in elementary, secondary and post-secondary education. This includes a major expansion of broadband availability in K-12 schools nationwide as well as an expansion in school construction.

Also, through the American Recovery and Reinvestment Act, he put $5 billion into early education, including Head Start.

He signed the Post-9/11 GI Bill, also known as GI Bill 2.0

He oversaw expansion of the Pell Grants program to expand opportunity for low-income students to go to college.

He passed the Individuals with Disabilities Education Act, which provided an extra $12.2 billion in funds.

Greater Transparency and Better Government

He signed an order banning gifts from lobbyists to anyone in the Executive Branch.

He signed an order banning anyone from working in an agency they had lobbied in previous years. He also put strict limits on lobbyists' access to the White House. He held the first-ever online town hall from the White House, and took questions from the public.

The Obama White House became the first to stream every White House event, live.

He established a central portal for Americans to find service opportunities.

He provided the first voluntary disclosure of the White House Visitors Log in history. He crafted an Executive Order on Presidential Records, which restored the 30-day time frame for former presidents to review records, and eliminated the right for the vice president or family members of former presidents to do the reviews. This will provide the public with greater access to historic White House documents, and severely curtails the ability to use executive privilege to shield them.

He improved aspects of the Freedom of Information Act, and issued new guidelines to make FOIA more open and transparent in the processing of FOIA requests.

National Safety and Security

He's restored federal agencies such as FEMA to the point that they have been able to manage a huge number of natural disasters successfully.

He authorized Navy SEALS to successfully secure the release of a US captain held by Somali pirates and increased patrols off the Somali coast.

Obama has repeatedly beefed up border security.

He ordered and oversaw the Navy SEALS operation that killed Osama bin Laden.

Science, Technology and Health Care

He created a Presidential Memorandum to restore scientific integrity in government decision-making.

Obama opened up the process for fast-tracking patent approval for green energy projects.

He eliminated the Bush-era restrictions on embryonic stem cell research. He also provided increased federal support for biomedical and stem cell research.

Through the American Recovery and Reinvestment Act, he committed more federal funding, about $18 billion, to support non-defense science and research labs.

He signed the Christopher and Dana Reeve Paralysis Act, the first comprehensive attempt to improve the lives of Americans living with paralysis.

He expanded the Nurse-Family Partnership program, which provides home visits by trained registered nurses to low-income expectant mothers and their families, to cover more first-time mothers. His EPA reversed research ethics standards which allowed humans to be used as "guinea pigs" in tests of the effects of chemicals to comply with numerous codes of medical ethics.

Obama conducted a cyberspace policy review.

Obama provided financial support for private sector space programs.

He oversaw enhanced earth mapping to provide valuable data for agricultural, educational, scientific, and government use.

He ushered through a bill that authorized the Food and Drug Administration to regulate tobacco products. As a result, the FDA has ordered tobacco companies to disclose cigarette ingredients and to ban sale of cigarettes falsely labeled as "light."

Through the American Recovery and Reinvestment Act, he provided $500 million for Health Professions Training Programs.

He also increased funding for community-based prevention programs. He oversaw a 50% decrease in cost of prescription drugs for seniors. He eliminated the Bush-era practice of forbidding Medicare from negotiating with drug companies on price.

Two weeks after taking office, he signed the Children's Health Insurance Re-authorization Act, which increased the number of children covered by health insurance by 4 million.

He held a quick press conference, and urged Congress to investigate Anthem Blue Cross for raising premiums 39% without explanation. Rep. Waxman responded by launching a probe, and Anthem Blue Cross put the increase on hold for two months.

He ushered through and signed the Affordable Health Care Act, which expanded health insurance coverage to 30 million more people, and ended many common insurance company practices that are often detrimental to those with coverage.

Through the Affordable Health Care Act, he allowed children to be covered under their parents' policy until they turned 26.

Through the Affordable Health Care Act, he provided tax breaks to allow 3.5 million small businesses to provide health insurance to their employees; thereby 29 million people will receive tax breaks to help them afford health insurance.

Through the Affordable Health Care Act, he expanded Medicaid to those making up to 133% of the federal poverty level.

Through the Affordable Health Care Act, health insurance companies now have to disclose how much of your premium actually goes to pay for patient care. Provisions in Obama's Affordable Health Care Act have already resulted in Medicare costs actually declining slightly this fiscal year, for the first time in many years, according to the Congressional Budget Office. Last year's increase was 4%. Compare that to the average 12% annual inflation rate during the previous 40 years.

Strengthening the Middle Class and Families

Obama worked to provide affordable, high-quality child care to working families.

He cracked down on companies that were previously denying sick pay, vacation and health insurance, and Social Security and Medicare tax payments through abuse of the employee classification of independent contractor. Through the American Recovery and Reinvestment Act, he cut taxes for 95% of America's working families. Under Obama, tax rates for average working families are the lowest they've been since 1950.

He extended and fully funded the patch for the Alternative Minimum Tax for 10 years.

He extended discounted COBRA health coverage for the unemployed from 9 months to 15 months, and he's extended unemployment benefits several times.

Environment and Energy

Obama created fast-tracked regulations to allow states to enact federal fuel efficiency standards that were above federal standards. His fast-tracked regulation increased fuel economy standards for vehicles beginning with the 2011 model year. It was the first time such standards had been increased in a decade.

He oversaw the establishment of an Energy Partnership for the Americas, which creates more markets for American-made biofuels and green energy technologies. His EPA reversed a Bush-era decision to allow the largest mountaintop removal project in US history.

He ordered the Department of Energy to implement more aggressive efficiency standards for common household appliances.

He ordered energy plants to prepare to produce at least 15% of all energy through renewable resources like wind and solar, by 2021. (As you can see, Republicans are trying hard to kill it.)

He oversaw the creation of an initiative that converts old factories and manufacturing centers into new clean technology centers.

Obama bypassed Republican opposition in Congress, and ordered EPA to begin regulating and measuring carbon emissions.

His EPA ruled that CO_2 is a pollutant.

He doubled federal spending on clean energy research.

He pushed through a tax credit to help people buy plug-in hybrid cars.

He created a program to develop renewable energy projects on the waters of our Outer Continental Shelf that will produce electricity from wind, wave, and ocean currents.

Obama reengaged in the climate change and greenhouse gas emissions agreements talks, and even proposed one himself. He also addressed the U.N. Climate Change Conference, officially reversing the Bush-era stance that climate change was a "hoax."

He fully supported the initial phase of the creation of a legally binding treaty to reduce mercury emissions worldwide. He required states to provide incentives to utilities to reduce their energy consumption.

Following Bush's eight year reign, he reengaged in a number of treaties and agreements designed to protect the Antarctic.

He created tax write-offs for purchases of hybrid automobiles, and later he and Democrats morphed that program into one that includes electric cars. Mandated that federal government fleet purchases be for fuel-efficient American vehicles, and encouraged that federal agencies support experimental, fuel-efficient vehicles.

Obama oversaw and pushed through an amendment to the Oil Pollution Act of 1990 authorizing advances from Oil Spill Liability Trust Fund for the Deepwater Horizon oil spill. He also actively tried to amend the Oil Pollution Act of 1990 to eliminate the liability limits for those companies responsible for large oil spills.

He initiated Criminal and Civil inquiries into the Deepwater Horizon oil spill. Through Obama's EPA, he asserted federal legal supremacy, and barred Texas from authorizing new refinery permits on its own. He strengthened the Endangered Species Act. His EPA improved boiler safety standards to improve air quality and save 6500 lives per year.

Through the EPA, he took steps to severely limit the use of antibiotics in livestock feed, and to increase their efficacy in humans. Obama increased funding for National Parks and Forests by 10%.

He announced greatly improved commercial fuel efficiency standards. He announced the development of a huge increase in average fuel economy standards from 27.5mpg to 35.5mpg starting in 2016 and 54.5 starting in 2025.

Other Accomplishments

Obama has expanded trade agreements to include stricter labor and environmental agreements such as NAFTA.

He oversaw funding of the design of a new Smithsonian National Museum of African-American History, which is scheduled to open on the National Mall in 2015. He protected the funding during the recent budget negotiations.

He oversaw and passed increased funding for the National Endowment for the Arts.

Obama nominated Sonia Sotomayor and Elena Kagan to the Supreme Court. Sotomayor is the first Hispanic Justice in the Court's history, and these women represent only the third and fourth women to serve on the court, out of a total of 112 justices. He appointed the most diverse Cabinet in history, including more women than any other incoming president. He eliminated federal funding for abstinence-only education, and he rescinded the global gag rule.

Obama loosened the rules, and allowed the 14 states that legalized medical marijuana to regulate themselves without federal interference. His FDA banned the use of antibiotics in livestock production. Obama ushered through and signed national service legislation, increasing funding for national service groups, including tripling the size of the AmeriCorps program.

The material used for the list of accomplishments was obtained from the article below. It has been altered somewhat due to many of the current events that have taken place globally in last few weeks and months.

Read the original article at http://pleasecutthecrap.typepad.com/main/what-has-obama-done-since-january-20-2009.html

Post Script

It is clear that President Obama is one of the most successful presidents of all time. Despite a much fractured Congress and a very disruptive Republican/Tea Party, President Barack Obama has exceeded all expectations as a president. Whoever the next president in 2016 is---one thing is for sure---she/he will definitely follow in the footstep of a presidential giant.

As an aside, I hope the voting public will evaluate the Republican/Tea Party in a fair and balanced manner. It should be based on the number of their accomplishments for the American people since President Bush left office. That evaluation should be very easy based on the overwhelming number of their accomplishments. At the last count Republicans/Tea Party have **ZERO ACCOMPLISHMENTS.**

If you really want to know which party to support in the upcoming presidential elections in fall 2016, just ask yourself one important question based on the following. Twenty one years ago the Republicans swept into office with their promise in 1994 of a *Contract with America.*

A November 13, 2000 article by Edward H. Crane, president of the libertarian Cato Institute, stated, "...the combined budgets of the 95 major programs that the Contract with America promised to eliminate have increased by 13%." President Bill Clinton often remarked that the Republicans had actually put forth a *"Contract on America."*

The question you need to ask yourself and answer is---What part of Contract with America, if any, was ever accomplished by the Republican Party? If the answer is none of it, then you should clearly know which party or candidates to support in the upcoming 2016 elections. Why, you ask? --- Because history, including political history, has a habit of repeating itself.

The government shutdown, and economic harm that was subsequently felt by the American people in 2013, was caused by Republican/Tea Party members in Congress. I think it is fair to say that any Republican/Tea Party members running in the 2016 elections (who supported the government shutdown) should have no subsequent role in that government since they tried to "deep six" the United States in 2013.

Chapter 2

The Tea Party in America:

Political Lunatic Fringe or New Face of the Republican Party?

Introduction

Historians will one day write about one of the greatest crises to face the United States Government. That crisis occurred just two years ago when the country was on a catastrophic train wreck to oblivion.

What happened was this: the government began to go into a tailspin with a partial shutdown of the U.S. government which included a catastrophic threat of financial default and ruin of the country's credit status. In addition, there was a threat that the nation's debt limit was not going to be extended beyond October 17, 2013. This chaos, in turn, would directly prevent the

U.S. government from paying its bills and meeting its financial obligations.

The following is an edited version of an Associated Press article:

"Standard & Poor's estimated the shutdown has taken $24 billion out of the economy, and the Fitch credit rating agency had warned that it was reviewing its AAA rating on U.S. government debt for a possible downgrade.

President Obama and his Democratic allies on Capitol Hill were the decisive victors in the fight, which was sparked by Tea Party Republicans including Sen. Ted Cruz of Texas. They prevailed upon skeptical GOP leaders to use a normally routine short-term funding bill in an attempt to "defund" the 2010 Affordable Health Care Law known as 'Obama care.'

'We fought the good fight. We just didn't win,' House Speaker John Boehner, R-Ohio, conceded. He was given positive reviews from Republicans for his handling of the crisis, though it again exposed the tenuous grasp he holds over the fractious House GOP conference. Republican Sen. John McCain of Arizona said the American people disapproved of how Republicans, and also Democrats and the president, handled the budget gridlock.

'Hopefully, the lesson is to stop this foolish childishness,' McCain said Thursday on CNN. The shutdown sent approval of the GOP plummeting in opinion polls and exasperated veteran lawmakers who saw it as folly. 'It's time to restore some sanity to this place,' House Appropriations Committee Chairman Harold Rogers, R-Ky., said before the vote.'[1]

Who Created the Economic Crisis?

The instigators of this crisis were a minority of congressmen in the House of Representatives representing just one political faction of the Republican Party. This political faction is known as the **Tea Party**.

---

[1] Associated Press Writers: Alan Fram, Jessica Gresko, and Connie Cass. "Government open again, Obama bemoans Damage", October 17, 2013

Public polls during the crisis overwhelmingly condemned the Republican Party in general for holding the country hostage. But the Tea Party, as instigators, was blamed even more for their reckless, irresponsible, failed and ill-conceived plan, that in15 days into the shutdown had already hurt a million+ people nationwide.

Initially, it was their plan to use the shutdown as a bargaining chip in their desire to force concessions on the Affordable Care Act, and to cut federal spending. And this misguided extremism via extortion was attempted as a strategy in lieu of the normal legislative process. Such a deleterious plan, approved and executed by the Tea Party, gives the distinct impression that Tea Party members are "**not-too-bright.**"

It's fair to say that Tea Party ultraconservatives are, as a result of their failure to implement a destructive financial meltdown and default of the United States government, earned the scorn of the American people, but are now the laughing stock of the nation. Because of Tea Party actions, the United States, at the very least, was embarrassed before the international community and our allies.

Now that the dust has settled (at least for a while in Washington D.C.) it's important to learn more about what the Tea Party is really all about. Are they dangerous individuals who need to be tried for treason? Are they right-wing ideologues representing the values of the most extremist conservative viewpoints giving a great portrayal of a lunatic fringe? Do they actually represent a threat to the American people?

And finally, should people who cavalierly took the nation to the near brink of financial ruin, harming millions of people in their wake, be held accountable and charged with criminal acts and eventually punished accordingly? These questions should now be asked by people in government, the FBI, and the United States Department of Justice.

But first it is important to ask a set of less dire questions to get a correct picture of who these people are, including those currently (but perhaps temporarily) holding office in the House of Representatives. Ultimately, one needs to assess the facts by asking a set of simple questions:

- **What is the Tea Party?**
- **What do they want?**
- **What are their Demographics?**
- **What's Public Opinion of the Tea Party?**
- **Who is Funding the Tea Party?**

What is the Tea Party?

The **Tea Party movement** is an American decentralized political movement that is primarily known for advocating a reduction in the U.S. National debt and federal budget deficit by reducing U.S. government spending and taxes. The movement has been called partly conservative, partly libertarian, and partly populist. It has sponsored protests and supported political candidates since 2009.

The name is derived from the Boston Tea Party of 1773, an iconic event in American history. Anti-tax protesters in the United States have often referred to the original Boston Tea Party for inspiration. References to the Boston Tea Party were part of Tax Day protests held throughout the 1990s and earlier. By 2001, a custom had developed among some conservative activists of mailing tea bags to legislators and other officials as a symbolic act.

What do they want?

The Tea Party does not have a single uniform agenda. The Tea Party generally focuses on government reform. Among its goals are limiting the size of the federal government, reducing government spending, lowering the national debt and opposing tax increases. To this end, Tea Party groups have protested the Troubled Asset Relief Program (TARP), stimulus programs such as the American Recovery and Reinvestment Act of 2009 (ARRA, commonly referred to as the Stimulus or The Recovery Act), cap and trade, health care reform such as the Patient Protection and Affordable Care Act (PPACA, also known simply as the Affordable Care Act or "Obama care") and perceived attacks by the federal government on their 1st, 2nd, 4th and 10th Amendment rights.

The decentralized character of the Tea Party, with its lack of formal structure or hierarchy, allows each autonomous group to set its own priorities and goals. Goals may conflict, and priorities will often differ between groups. Many Tea Party organizers see this as strength rather than a weakness, as decentralization has helped to immunize the Tea Party against co-opting by outside entities and corruption from within.

The Tea Party has generally sought to avoid placing too much emphasis on traditional conservative social issues. National Tea Party organizations, such as the Tea Party Patriots and Freedom Works, have expressed concern that engaging in social issues would be divisive. Instead, they have sought to have activists focus their efforts away from social issues and focus on economic and limited government issues. Still, many groups like Glenn Beck's 9/12 Tea Parties, TeaParty.org, the Iowa Tea Party and Delaware Patriot Organizations do act on social issues such as abortion, gun control, prayer in schools, and illegal immigration.

Tea Party groups have also voiced support for right to work legislation as well as tighter border security, and opposed amnesty for illegal immigrants. After the Republican Party lost seats in Congress and the Presidency in the 2012 elections, they began to work at the state level to nullify the healthcare reform law.

They have also protested the IRS for controversial treatment of groups with "tea party" in their names. They have formed

Super Pac's to support candidates sympathetic to their goals, and have opposed what they call the "Republican establishment" candidates.

Even though the groups have a wide range of goals, the Tea Party places the Constitution at the center of its reform agenda. It urges the return of government as intended by the Founding Fathers.

It also seeks to teach its view of the Constitution and other founding documents. Scholars have described its interpretation variously as originalist, popular, or a unique combination of the two. However, their reliance on the Constitution is selective and inconsistent. Adherents cite it, yet do so more as a cultural reference rather than out of commitment to the text, which they seek to alter.

Several constitutional amendments have been targeted by some in the movement for full or partial repeal, including the 14th, 16th, and 17th. There has also been support for a proposed Repeal Amendment, which would enable a two-thirds majority of the states to repeal federal laws, and a Balanced Budget Amendment, which would limit deficit spending. Had the United States had such an amendment during World War II, the U.S. would have lost that war.

One attempt at forming a list of what Tea Partiers wanted Congress to do was the basis of the *Contract from America*. It was a legislative agenda created by conservative activist Ryan Hecker with the assistance of Dick Armey of Freedom Works. Armey had co-written the previous *Contract with America* released by the Republican Party during the 1994 midterm elections.

One thousand agenda ideas that had been submitted were narrowed down to twenty-one non-social issues. Participants then voted in an online campaign in which they were asked to select their favorite policy planks. The results were released as a ten-point Tea Party platform. The Contract from America was met with some support within the Republican Party, but it was not broadly embraced by GOP leadership, which released its own 'Pledge to America.'

What Are Their Demographics?

The vast majority of the Tea Party Caucus comes from the West and the South. Whether by accident or design, the public faces of the Tea Party in the House of Representatives are Midwesterners.

But while there may be Tea Party sympathizers throughout the country in the House of Representatives, the Tea Party faction alone used the debt ceiling issue to plunge the nation into crisis. Overwhelmingly this faction is Southern in its origins.

Sam Stein of the Washington Post wrote an interesting article called: *Tea Party Survey: Old, Conservative, Hate Obama, and Like Fox News*.

According to Sam Stein:

"The individuals who make up the Tea Party movement are largely conservative and get their news from Fox; they're generally old and of moderate to low income; and they're fairly convinced that their taxes are going to rise in the next few years, even though they likely won't.

Those conclusions are part of a new study put together by The Winston Group, a conservative-leaning polling and strategy firm run by the former director of planning for former Speaker of the House Newt Gingrich. And they provide a telling new window on the political force that has revamped the Republican Party and altered the landscape of the 2010 elections.

In the course of conducting three national surveys of 1,000 registered voters, Winston was able to peg the percentage of the public that identifies itself with the Tea Party at roughly 17 percent. The group pledges that it is independent of any particular party (indeed 28 percent of Tea Party respondents in the Winston survey labeled their affiliation as such). But on pretty much every defining political or demographic issue, the movement lines up with the GOP or conservative alternatives.

Sixty-five percent of Tea Party respondents called themselves 'conservative' compared to the 33 percent of all respondents who did the same. Just eight percent of Tea Party respondents said they were 'liberal.'"

Forty-seven percent of Tea Party respondents said that Fox News was either the top or second source of news they turn to, compared with 19 percent of the overall public who said the same thing.

More than 80 percent (81 percent) of Tea Party respondents expressed very little approval of Barack Obama's job as President, which exceeded disapproval levels held even by Republicans (77%) and conservatives (79%).

All these data points suggest that the Tea Party crowd is comprised predominantly of conservatives. And, not surprisingly, the demographics of the movement seemingly align with those who traditionally vote for the conservative candidate as well. Fifty-six percent of Tea Party respondents are male; 22 percent are over the age of 65 (compared with just 14 percent who are between the ages of 18 and 34); and 23 percent fall in the income range of $50,000 and $75,000.

In another survey, Tea Party supporters are likely to be *older, white and male.* Forty percent are age 55 and over, compared with 32 percent of all poll respondents; just 22 percent are under the age of 35, 79 percent are white, and 61 percent are men. Many are also Christian fundamentalists, with 44 percent identifying themselves as "born-again," compared with 33 percent of all respondents."

The Tea Party Members in Congress

Fiery Republicans known as the Tea Party Caucus are at the center of the debate over which version of a plan - if any - to cut spending and raise the debt limit should be adopted in Congress.

These conservatives, many of whom were swept into office during the 2010 midterm elections, have made it their mission to rein in spending and shrink the size of government, even if it meant taking the country to the edge of default.

Here is the full list of the official Tea Party Caucus in the House of Representatives, with the freshman representatives in **BOLD**:

Sandy Adams (FL-24)
Robert Aderholt (AL-04)
Todd Akin (MO-02)
Rodney Alexander (LA-05)
Michele Bachmann (MN-06)
Roscoe Bartlett (MD-06)
Joe Barton (TX-06)
Rob Bishop (UT-01)
Gus Bilirakis (FL-09)
Diane Black (TN-06)
Paul Broun (GA-10)
Michael Burgess (TX-26)
Dan Burton (IN-05)

John Carter (TX-31)
Bill Cassidy (LA-06)
Howard Coble (NC-06)
Mike Coffman (CO-06)
Ander Crenshaw (FL-04)
John Culberson (TX-07)
Jeff Duncan (SC-03)
Blake Farenthold (TX-27)
Stephen Lee Fincher (TN-08)
John Fleming (LA-04)
Trent Franks (AZ-02)
Phil Gingrey (GA-11)
Louie Gohmert (TX-01)
Vicky Hartzler (MO-04)
Wally Herger (CA-02)
Tim Huelskamp (KS-01)
Lynn Jenkins (KS-02)
Steve King (IA-05)
Doug Lamborn (CO-05)
Jeff Landry (LA-03)
Blaine Luetkemeyer (MO-09)
Kenny Marchant (TX-24)
Tom McClintock (CA-04)
David McKinley (WV-01)
Gary Miller (CA-42)
Mick Mulvaney (SC-05)
Randy Neugebauer (TX-19)

Rich Nugent (FL-05)
Steven Palazzo (MS-04)
Steve Pearce (NM-02)
Mike Pence (IN-06)
Ted Poe (TX-02)
Tom Price (GA-06)
Denny Rehberg (MT-At large)
David Roe (TN-01)
Dennis Ross (FL-12)
Edward Royce (CA-40)
Steve Scalise (LA-01)
Pete Sessions (TX-32)
Adrian Smith (NE-03)
Lamar Smith (TX-21)
Cliff Stearns (FL-06)
Tim Walberg (MI-07)
Joe Walsh (IL-08)
Allen West (FL-22)
Lynn Westmoreland (GA-03)
Joe Wilson (SC-02)

What's Public Opinion of the Tea Party?

The Tea Party is more unpopular than ever before, according to a Rasmussen poll recently released, with just three in 10 voters holding favorable views of the movement. Half of respondents said they view the party unfavorably. The Rasmussen survey used automated phone calls to survey 1,000 likely voters back in January.

The numbers obtained in the survey represented a considerable dive in support since the Tea Party's heyday in 2009, when a majority of voters rated it favorably.

Many of the Senate challengers with Tea Party backing were defeated in 2012, and the movement suffered another PR blow after a falling out among the leadership of the Tea Party group, Freedom Works.

Although most members of the House's Tea Party Caucus were reelected in November, the group had some high-profile losses, including the defeats of former Reps. Joe Walsh and Allen West.

Rep. Michele Bachmann (R-Minn.), the chairwoman of the House Tea Party Caucus, barely retained her seat.

The movement is now widely seen by the public as declining, according to the Rasmussen poll -- 56 percent of voters said the Tea Party became less influential over the past year, and just 8 percent said they identified as part of the Tea Party movement.

Other polling conducted since the election has found similar results when looking at the Tea Party's popularity, but with a larger number of people saying they agreed with or were part of the movement. A CNN/ORC poll conducted in November last year found that half of Americans viewed the Tea Party unfavorably; actually a modest improvement from the movement's standing in late 2011.

A December poll from Politico/GWU found that 21 percent of likely voters identified with or considered themselves part of the Tea Party movement. Polls from CNBC in November both found that about

20 percent of adults were supporters of the movement.

In an article by Carol Forsloff titled, **"Tea Party Demographics: White, Republican, Older Male with Money"** reported:

"Several polls are now out, assessing the demographics of the Tea Party Movement that largely agree the majority of its members are Republican, largely white, above the mean in age and income and voted for John McCain.

So do Tea Party people reflect the average American as they represent themselves? Not usually if you are a middle-aged woman of Hispanic background, an African-American male or a union member in New England just scraping by, according to the polls."

A conservative blogger examined this analysis of Tea Party members, citing CNN statistics declaring they are predominantly male, more college educated and higher earners than the general population at large, but not necessarily older or just from the

South. A progressive blogger on Think Progress looked at the CNN statistics and relayed the same information as the conservative fellow, stating the following:

"Turns out that the 'tea party' movement sweeping the nation is disproportionately composed of individuals who have higher-than-average incomes. It's also disproportionately composed of men. And disproportionately composed of white people. And, disproportionately composed of self-identified conservatives. And, disproportionately composed of self-identified Republicans. In other words, well-to-do conservative white men don't much care for Barack Obama's policies. Which, of course, is something we already knew from the exit polls back in November 2008?"

Who is Funding the Tea Party?

In an August 30, 2010, article in The New Yorker, Jane Mayer said that the billionaire brothers David H. Koch and Charles G. Koch and Koch Industries are providing financial and organizational support to the Tea Party movement through Americans for Prosperity, which David founded. The AFP's "Hot Air Tour" was organized to fight against taxes on carbon use and the activation of a cap and trade program.

In 1984, David Koch also founded Citizens for a Sound Economy, part of which became Freedom Works in a 2004 split, another group that organized and supports the movement.

Koch Industries issued a press release stating that the Koch's have "no ties to and have never given money to Freedom Works". Former ambassador Christopher Meyer wrote in the Daily Mail that the Tea Party movement is a mix of "grassroots populism, professional conservative politics, and big money", the last supplied in part by the Koch's. Mayer says that the Koch brothers' political involvement with the Tea Party has been so secretive that she labels it "covert."

Post Script

Many organizations in society, including political organizations, engage in what is called sub- optimizing behavior. That's when stated goals are not the real goals; they are simply stated goals.

The real goals of organizations, political groups, or individuals are often hidden and not stated publicly. Words from politicians often disguise their real motives. Beliefs and values dominate all our lives. And the Tea Party is no exception, especially when backed by Big Business and the Billionaire Koch Brothers and Koch Industries.

Based on the behavior of Tea Party members in Congress, **my assumption these last few weeks is that the Tea Party in America is both a lunatic fringe and the new face of the Republican Party.**

Currently only 8% of Americans identify themselves as Tea Party members. And, it appears the Tea Party

in Congress has a stranglehold on other Republicans.

It's okay for people to cling to their values and beliefs. But when such values and beliefs threaten the United States with financial disaster and ruin, then it's time for other stronger forces to counter such attacks on the integrity of the United States and its people.

As much as I'd like to see it, it's unlikely these congressional reprobates will ever be tried for treason or brought up on criminal charges by the U.S. Department of Justice. The best thing the people can do is toss the Tea Party members out of Congress in the next election. Another option is to petition their immediate recall from office.

The Ongoing Problem of Gridlock

The vast majority of Americans are moderate "Middle-of-the-Road" Independents, Democrats and Republicans. When one has different values from their fellow citizens, it naturally creates tension, suspicion, distrust, and polarization.

Since 2008 we've witnessed the worst of these political differences acting out as irreconcilable gridlock when it comes to carrying out the various duties of the government (passing a budget on time, passing legislation to help our citizens, properly defending the country, etc.). For several years now gridlock has created and prevented very little from being accomplished.

Politics has always been called, "the Art of Compromise." This is an old saying that no longer appears applicable in modern day politics.

The primary function of politicians should be to honestly represent their constituency. But at the same time politicians need to make prudent, critical choices in the handling of scarce resources (taxpayer dollars). That latter function is an awesome responsibility that needs careful attention to detail. But the overriding responsibility of those in Congress today should be to help their fellow citizens live better, more prosperous lives.

Unfortunately, the legacy of conservatism or radical conservatism has never aligned itself with helping people. During the last 160 years, conservatives were opposed to the abolition of slavery, fought against giving women the right to vote, fought against integration, desegregation and later busing, opposed the New Deal during the Depression of the 1930s, opposed the Social Security Act in 1935 and later, minimum wage laws. They were a major voice against the Civil Rights Movement of the 1960s, and were responsible for promoting racism and Jim Crow, particularly in the old South. During the 1970s conservatives also opposed affirmative action.

In more recent years, conservatives have opposed amnesty for illegal aliens. They also want to cut entitlement programs like Social Security and Medicare, and now their strident attitude is to oppose the President's Affordable Care Act that promotes universal healthcare. One way of characterizing all this political history is that, if legislation was going to help a lot people and improve their lives, conservatives were "hell-bent" to oppose it.

At this point in history the Tea Party has been at the center of Washington's gridlock. The only real option for Americans in the 2016 national elections is to terminate Tea Party conservatives and most Republicans from holding office in the United States Congress.

This doesn't mean that creating jobs, cutting spending or raising or lowering taxes aren't important issues; they certainly are. But Tea Party members who take a simplistic ideological viewpoint of how the economy works lack insight into the complexities of the economy and its business cycles.

Just remember the following statistics:

"Since Democrat John F. Kennedy took office in January 1961, non-government payrolls in the U.S. swelled by almost 42 million jobs under Democrats, compared with 24 million for Republican presidents, according to Labor Department figures. Democrats hold the edge though they occupied the Oval Office for 23 years since Kennedy's inauguration, compared with 28 for the Republicans. In addition, over the past 50 years, Republican administrations oversaw the largest decline in wages as measured as a percentage of the U.S. Gross Domestic Product (GDP).

If you really care about data and facts (not just value judgments), then it should be very clear to you who to vote for during the 2016 elections."

Chapter 3

The 2014 Midterm Elections

The Future of the Republican Party

In America

Introduction

The upcoming 2014 Mid-term elections will be one of the most important in American political history. This is because we, as Americans, are coming to a crossroads as far as where we want the country to go in the future. After six years of gridlock, the country as a whole is fed-up with politicians. This anger the public feels might be translated into a larger voter turnout in November or not (people staying home on Election Day).

At the moment I can't predict which way that might go. Efforts to get people to vote will be critical in this mid-term election. Traditionally, weak voter turnout occurs in mid-term elections more than in years where both parties are running candidates for President.

However, the country has placed more blame on the Republican Party and their Tea Party sidekicks for the debilitating government shutdown that occurred in late 2013. Consequently, the probability that many Republicans and Tea Party members will be re-elected to the House or Senate in 2014 is slim to none. I base this prediction on four major factors:

- Changing Ethnic and Racial Demographics

- The Tea Party in America: Gridlock and the Legacy of Conservatism

- Age-Related Generational Perspectives

- Hypocrisy of Republican Political Values (smaller government and lower taxes)

Changing Ethnic and Racial Demographics

One reason it is difficult to predict elections is something called *changing demographics.*

Early evidence suggests that, based on changing demographics, *The Republican Party* is fast on the track to becoming a defunct political party in the United States. It is conceivable that one day soon there may be just two major parties in the United States: *The Democratic Party* and perhaps an *Independent Party*. The more ethnically and racially diverse a political party is, the more likely they will receive a greater number of votes during election time.

The following information was obtained on the Internet by writer Frank Newport. Please notice the lack of diversity in the Republican Party.

PRINCETON, NJ -- Non-Hispanic whites accounted for 89% of Republican self-identifiers nationwide in 2012, while accounting for 70% of independents and 60% of Democrats. Over one-fifth of Democrats (22%) were black, while 16% of independents were Hispanic.

These results are based on more than 338,000 interviews conducted as part of Gallup Daily tracking in 2012, and clearly underscore the distinct racial profiles of partisan groups in today's political landscape.

- Republicans are overwhelmingly non-Hispanic white, at a level that is significantly higher than the self-identified white percentage of the national adult population. Just 2% of

Republicans are black, and 6% are Hispanic.

- Seventy percent of Americans who identify as independents are white, but independents have the highest representation of Hispanics (16%) of the three groups. Eight percent of independents are blacks.

- Democrats remain a majority white party, but four in 10 Democrats are something other than non-Hispanic white. More than one in five Democrats is black, roughly twice the black representation in the adult population.

Racial and Ethnic Groups Gravitate Toward Different Parties

Looked at differently, these party composition patterns reflect major differences in the way Americans in various racial and ethnic groups identify their political affiliation.

- Almost two-thirds of blacks identify as Democrats, with most of the rest identifying as independents. Only 5% of blacks nationwide identify as Republicans.

- Half of Hispanics identify as independents, although the majority of the rest identify as Democrats. This is despite their high level of approval and strong majority voting support for Democratic President Barack Obama. Relatively few Hispanics (6%) identify as Republicans.

- Whites are the most politically diverse of the three major racial and ethnic segments, with between 26% and 38% identifying with one of the three partisan groups. Whites tilt slightly toward being independents or

Republicans rather than Democrats. The large white concentration of Republican identifiers, in short, is caused by a dearth of nonwhites self-identifying with the GOP, rather than a monolithic Republican orientation among whites.

Although Asians and other races make up a small proportion of the U.S. population, the data show that the political pattern they follow is quite similar to that of Hispanics: they are most likely to identify as independents, second-most likely to identify as Democrats, and least likely to identify as Republicans.

Racial Breakdown of Independents and Democrats Has Shifted Most Since 2008

The racial and ethnic composition of the Republican Party today is similar to what it was in 2008, the year when Gallup began its daily tracking. There have been essentially no changes in the percentage of

GOP identifiers who are white, black, and Hispanic.

Independents have become more Hispanic since 2008 (and slightly more black), while Democrats have become more black and more Hispanic. Phrased differently, the independent and Democratic segments of the U.S. population are now less white than they were in 2008, reflecting the uptick in the U.S. nonwhite population over these five years.

Implications

One of the more important realities in American politics today is the substantial divergence in the racial and ethnic composition of the major political parties. Almost nine in 10 Republicans are white, in stark contrast to the racial and ethnic composition of the overall adult population. On the other hand, the Democratic Party is disproportionately nonwhite.

The future of the two major political parties depends on two factors. The first is whether these patterns of party identification change in the years ahead. The ability of the Republican Party to make inroads among nonwhites has been much discussed in recent months, particularly the GOP's efforts to improve on the 13% allegiance that Gallup data show it obtains from Hispanics. Another path to growth for the Republican Party would be an increase in its penetration into the white sector of the population, only 35% of which now identifies as Republican. On the other hand, the Democratic Party will grow if it too can extend its identification among whites, and maintain or strengthen its position among nonwhites.

A second factor that will affect the future of the political parties in the U.S. is straightforward demographics. Projections show that the nonwhite proportion of the American adult population will grow in the years ahead. This means that if current partisan allegiance patterns prevail, the size of the Democratic base will be in a better position to grow than will the Republican base.

The Tea Party in America: Gridlock and the Legacy of Conservatism

Many organizations in society, including political organizations, engage in what is called sub-optimizing behavior. That's when stated goals are not the real goals.

The real goals of organizations, political groups, or individuals are often hidden and not stated publicly. Words from politicians often disguise their real motives. The Tea Party is no exception, especially when backed by Big Business and the Billionaire Koch Brothers and Koch Industries.

Based on the behavior of Tea Party members in Congress, my assumption is that the Tea Party in America is a lunatic fringe and, at the same time, is the new face of the Republican Party.

Currently only 8% of Americans identify themselves as Tea Party members. Nevertheless, the Tea Party in Congress has a stranglehold on all other Republicans. It's okay for people to cling to their values and beliefs. But when such values and beliefs threaten the United States with financial disaster and ruin, then it's time for other stronger forces to counter such attacks on the integrity of the United States and its people.

As much as I'd like to see it, it's unlikely these congressional reprobates will ever be tried for treason or brought up on criminal charges by the U.S. Department of Justice. The best thing the people can do is toss the Tea Party members out of Congress in the next election. Another option is to petition their immediate recall from office.

The Ongoing Problem of Gridlock

The vast majority of Americans are moderate "Middle-of-the-Road" independents, Democrats and Republicans. When one has different values from their fellow citizens, it naturally creates tension, suspicion, distrust, and polarization. Since 2008 we've witnessed the worst of these political differences acting out as irreconcilable gridlock when it comes to carrying out the various duties of the government (passing a budget on time, passing legislation to help our citizens, properly defending the country, etc.). For several years now, gridlock has created and prevented very little from being accomplished.

Politics has always been called, "the Art of Compromise." This is an old saying that no longer appears applicable in modern day politics.

The primary function of politicians should be to honestly represent their constituency. But at the same time politicians need to make prudent, critical choices in the handling of scarce resources (taxpayer dollars). That latter function is an awesome responsibility that needs careful attention to detail. But the overriding responsibility of those in Congress today should be to help their fellow citizens live better, more prosperous lives. With the exception of President Barack Obama, that does not seem to be the case.

The Legacy of Conservatism

Unfortunately, the legacy of conservatism has never aligned itself with helping people.

During the last 160 years conservatives were opposed to the abolition of slavery, and were responsible for promoting racism and Jim Crow, particularly in the old South. They fought against giving women the right to vote, opposed the New Deal during the Depression of the 1930s, and opposed the Social Security Act in 1935 and later, minimum wage laws. In the 1950s they fought against integration, desegregation and later busing. Conservatives were a major voice against the Civil Rights Movement of the 1960s; during the 1970s conservatives opposed affirmative action and the proposed Equal Rights Amendment.

In more recent years, conservatives have opposed amnesty for illegal aliens, and they want to cut entitlement programs like Social Security and Medicare. Now, with strong Tea Party support and a strident attitude, they oppose the President's Affordable Care Act that promotes universal healthcare.

One way of characterizing all this political history is that, if legislation was going to help a lot of people and improve their lives, conservatives were "hell-bent" to oppose it. That collectively is their ugly legacy.

At this point in history the Tea Party has been at the center of Washington's gridlock. The only real option for Americans in the 2016 national elections is to totally limit their access to power. This also applies to all Republicans seeking public office in the mid-term elections, and in 2016 as well.

This doesn't mean that creating jobs, cutting spending or raising or lowering taxes aren't important issues; they certainly are. But Tea Party members who take a simplistic ideological viewpoint of how the economy works lack insight into the complexities of the economy and its basic business cycles.

Come the Next Election Just Remember These Statistics

Since Democrat John F. Kennedy took office in January 1961, non-government payrolls in the U.S. swelled by almost 42 million jobs under Democrats, compared with 24 million for Republican presidents, according to Labor Department figures. Though they occupied the oval office for 23 years since Kennedy's inauguration, Democrats hold the edge, compared to 28 years for Republicans. In addition, over the past 50 years, Republican administrations oversaw the largest decline in wages as measured as a percentage of the U.S. Gross Domestic Product (GDP).

Age-Related Generational Issues

It has long been said that "our children are our future." And, given the fact that political perspectives vary by generation, it is incumbent upon society in general to recognize that voting patterns among the various generations will be very important to the future of politics in America. Nowhere is this truer than with the Millennial Generation. So what can we expect to happen in future elections? The following is a fine article written by Jonathan Chait. He refers to the Millennials as *"those kids with Obama posters on the wall."*

The Millennial Generation: Our Liberal Future

How doomed are conservatives? Pretty doomed if you look carefully at the Pew Research Survey's close analysis of the youth vote in the 2012 elections. The Republicans' long-term dilemma has generally been framed in racial terms, but it's mainly a generational one.

The youngest generation of voters contains a much smaller proportion of white voters than previous generations, and those whites in that generation vote Republican by a much smaller margin than their elders. What's more, younger voters supported President Obama during the last two election cycles for reasons that seem to go beyond the usual reasons — social issues like gay marriage and feminism, immigration policy, or Obama's personal appeal — and suggest a deeper attachment to liberalism. The proclivities of younger voters may actually portend a full-scale sea change in American politics.

More than four decades ago, Lloyd Free and Hadley Cantril identified the core of Americans' political thinking as a blend of symbolic conservatism and operational liberalism. Most Americans, that is, oppose big government in the abstract but favor it in the particular. They oppose "regulation" and "spending," but favor, say, enforcement of clean-air laws and Social Security. The push and pull between these contradictory beliefs has defined most of the political conflicts over the last century. Public support for most of the particulars of government has stopped Republicans from rolling back the advances of the New Deal, but suspicion with "big government" has made Democratic attempts to advance the role of the state rare and politically painful.

This tension continues to define the beliefs of American voters. Among the 2012 electorate, more voters identified themselves as conservative (35 percent) than liberal (25 percent), and more said the government is already doing too much that should be left to the private sector (51 percent) than asserted that the government ought to be doing more to solve problems (44 percent). But this is *not* the case with younger voters. By a 59 percent to 37 percent margin, voters under 30 say the government should do more to solve problems. More remarkably, 33 percent of voters under 30 identified themselves as liberal, as against 26 percent who called themselves conservative.

What all this suggests is that we may soon see a political landscape that will appear from the perspective of today and virtually all of American history as unrecognizably liberal. Democrats today must amass huge majorities of moderate voters in order to overcome conservatives' numerical advantage over liberals. They must carefully wrap any proposal for activist government within the strictures of limited government, which is why Bill Clinton declared the era of big government to be over, and Obama has promised not to raise taxes for 99 percent of Americans. It's entirely possible that, by the time today's twenty something's have reached middle age, these sorts of limits will cease to apply.

Obviously, such a future hinges on the generational patterns of the last two election cycles persisting. But, as another Pew survey showed, generational patterns do tend to be sticky. It's not the case that voters start out liberal and move rightward. Americans form a voting pattern early in their life and tend to hold to it. That isn't to say something couldn't shake these voters loose from their attachment to the liberal worldview. Republicans fervently (and plausibly) hoped the Great Recession would be that thing; having voted for Obama and borne the brunt of mass unemployment, once-idealistic voters would stare at the faded Obama posters on their wall and accept the Republican analysis that failed Big Government policies have brought about their misery.

But young voters haven't drawn this conclusion — or not many of them have, at any rate. So either something else is going to have to happen to disrupt the liberalism of the rising youth cohort, or else the Republican Party itself will have to change in ways far more dramatic than any of its leading lights seem prepared to contemplate.

Hypocrisy of Republican Political Values (smaller government and lower taxes)

The following is an interesting article that was posted on AlterNet on September 20, 2014 by Alex Henderson.

10 Red States that Mooch off the Federal Government

Republicans claim they've had it with American socialism. Maybe they should return the tax dollars subsidizing them.

One of the most hilarious talking points coming from far-right Republicans and the

Tea Party is that when "red states" like Mississippi, Alabama and Louisiana are asked to bail out California or Massachusetts, that's when they will finally become "fed up with socialism" and secede from the Union once and for all.

The problem with that meme is that it has no basis in reality: the more prosperous and Democrat-leaning areas of the United States are likely to be subsidizing dysfunctional "red states," many of which are suffering from insufficient tax revenue and an abundance of low-wage workers who don't have much to tax.

Tea Party Republicans like to point out that poor cities like Detroit, Baltimore and Camden, New Jersey are run by Democrats, but they neglect to mention that some of the most affluent parts of the United States— from Manhattan to the Silicon Valley and the San Francisco Bay Area to Cambridge, MA to Seattle to Chicago's North Shore suburbs—are dominated by the Democratic Party. People in those heavily Democratic areas pay a lot of federal income taxes, and quite often, their tax dollars go to red states.

Earlier this year, the personal finance website WalletHub.com conducted an in-depth study of the amounts individual states are paying in federal taxes compared to the amounts they are receiving. WalletHub analyzed data from the Internal Revenue Service, the U.S. Census Bureau, the U.S. Commerce Department and the Bureau of Labor Statistics. WalletHub's research demonstrates that, as a rule, the states that are the most likely to rail against "big government" are the most likely to be benefiting from it.

A few of the states in WalletHub's study that were receiving the most tax revenue from the federal government are states that President Barack Obama won in 2012 (most notably, New Mexico and Hawaii), but most were hardcore "red states." And most of the states that, according to WalletHub, are taking less from the federal government than they are paying in are "blue states" that Obama won in both 2008 and 2012, including California, Massachusetts, Delaware, Illinois, New Jersey, New York and Minnesota. WalletHub's research bears out comparable figures released by the nonpartisan Tax Foundation in the past: analyzing IRS data, Tax Foundation has found, more than once, that red states are likely to be the biggest recipients of federal tax money.

Summary and Conclusions

Back in the late 1960s I used to vote for liberal democrats and sometimes well-meaning moderate republicans, particularly in local elections. Moderate republicans today, unfortunately, are only a thing of the past. In 2000 when Al Gore was cheated out of becoming President of the United States, I knew it was time to close the chapter on ever voting for a republican again. Today, politics seems to be more about ideology than doing what's right for the country.

The Republican Party, along with its bastardized Tea Party, is a national disgrace to the people of the United States. With changing racial and ethnic demographics they are fast becoming defunct as a political party. Many factors have and will contribute to their demise:

- gridlock and the shutting down of the government in 2013 caused by a recalcitrant and belligerent Republican Party and their Tea Party affiliates in Congress

- a legacy of conservatism that has shamed the people of the United States in the eyes of the world

- the hypocrisy of their own values regarding the size of government and lowering taxes

- changing racial and ethnic demographics

- Generational changes in voting patterns

Republican and Tea Party members everywhere have no business representing anyone, anywhere, anytime. **It's time to get the country moving forward again. Please remember to vote in the 2016 national elections. It is critical that you do.**

Chapter 4

The Arrogance of Power

[The Vile History of the CIA and Crimes against Humanity]

PRES. BARACK OBAMA, UNITED STATES: The British, during World War II, when London was being bombed to smithereens had 200 or so detainees. And Churchill said, "We don't torture." Churchill understood: you start taking short-cuts, and over time, that corrodes what's—what's best in the people. It corrodes the character of a country.

Keith Olbermann show, 2009

Introduction

The people of the United States are at a crossroads of morality and conscience where torture policy in America is concerned. Much harm has been done to the reputation of this country as a civilized people, due to the expediency of policies during the Bush Administration believed to aid and assist the job of National Security. A secret policy of torture was promoted by the Bush Administration ostensibly to counter international terrorism. Subsequently, every "MOW-RON" and his brother came out of the woodwork to euphemistically describe torture as, "Enhanced Interrogation Techniques."

While it's one thing for a misguided, uneducated general public to miss the historical, religious, social, legal, sociological and psychological basis for prohibiting torture, there really is no excuse for former members of the government to do so, many of whom knew it was wrong from the start.

In recent weeks, the primary motivation of former Vice-President Dick Cheney, and others who promoted an after-the-fact dismissal of national and international law, including the Geneva Convention, was self-preservation, and the fear that they might one day soon be prosecuted and incarcerated for *crimes against humanity.*

Since we now have President George W. Bush's confession on tape, broadcast on the Keith Olbermann MSNBC show in 2009, the country knows that there was approval at the highest levels of government to commit these war crimes. Those guilty of war crimes did reach all the way from "lackey" levels in the CIA to military prisons in Iraq and elsewhere, and finally to the Bush White House itself.

More blatant rationalizations came recently from ex-vice president Dick Cheney. He appears on the television networks as the primary defender of torture. Cheney, who never went beyond his freshman year of college, seems to lack any understanding of law and shows absolutely no remorse for initiating and promoting torture and *crimes against humanity*.

How soon do the American people forget history? At the end of World War II many public servants, low-level bureaucrats, military officers, Nazi SS elite, judges, and high-level government officials were brought to the Nuremburg War Crimes Tribunal and tried for crimes against humanity. Where German military and concentration guards were concerned, they were not allowed to defend themselves with rationalizations like "We were only following orders," or "let's put this all behind us and look to the future" (sound familiar?). The Japanese also were tried after WWII for war crimes, including those who used waterboarding to torture prisoners. Many were sentenced and put to death by hanging for **Crimes against Humanity**.

Crimes against humanity were viewed as great violations of this country's values to respect life and humanity in general. Policies of torture rob our nation of both dignity and respect. If we fail to act responsibly now as a nation, and fail to bring to justice all those involved in initiating an American torture policy or promoting or carrying out war crimes in the name of the United States, the consequences of a dishonored nation with a double standard will taint the American image, and thus taint the American people forever more. According to Alfred W. McCoy in his important book, *A Question of Torture: CIA Interrogation, from the Cold War to the War on Terror,* concluded:

> "Finally, as we learned from France's battle for Algiers in the 1950s and Britain's Northern Ireland conflict in the 1970s, a nation that sanctions torture in defiance of democratic

principles pays a terrible price. For nearly two millennia, the practice has been identified with tyrants and empires. For the past two centuries, its repudiation has been synonymous with the humanist ideals of the Enlightenment and democracy. When any modern state tortures even a few victims, the stigma compromises its majesty and corrupts its integrity. Its officials must spin an even more complex web of lies that, in the end, weakens the bonds of trust and the rule of law that are the sine qua non of a democracy. And, beyond its borders, allies and enemies turn away in collective revulsion."

Background

The Central Intelligence Agency (CIA) has been involved in torture, kidnapping, extortion, blackmail and murder since its official inception in 1947 when the CIA was organized from its predecessor, *The OSS--- Office of Strategic Services*. Both agencies have had a *long* and *vile* history. Individuals responsible for these violations of national and international law have never been held accountable because of the veil of secrecy and the alleged compromise to American intelligence gathering and national security. Because of this the public ends up not knowing whether the CIA did their clandestine activities out of a legitimate need for protecting the nation's security, or was it a bogus smokescreen to cover up criminal behavior, including murders committed on behalf of the agency?

With more and more revelations every day that the CIA engaged in a long rogue program of illegal activity bordering on treason (any act of betrayal or disloyalty)--- in this case the undermining of the laws, values and ideals of the American people, it is imperative that the crimes not be stonewalled or met with impunity.

In addition, the violation of civil and human rights (decade after decade) warrants a long overdue charge of "**Crimes Against Humanity**" directed at individuals responsible including the chief architects of such programs.

It is now clear that in order to regain any shred of national respect and honor in the eyes of the American people and the rest of the world, those responsible must finally be brought to justice. Such vile human conduct of the last 72 years must not be *whitewashed* or swept under the *rug of obscurity*. The CIA has castrated the Declaration of Human Rights worldwide and, at home, stripped all moral authority of the United States to promote human rights anywhere in the world.

The CIA has used mind control drugs on unwitting experimental subjects, been a party to, over the last seventy two years, the murder or attempted murder of international democratically-elected political figures, and has been directly involved in training 56,000 South American soldiers (School of the Americas at Fort Benning, Georgia) in methods of torture. Torture methods taught were eventually used against innocent civilians (men, women and children), political figures, militant rebels, and military combatants and detainees, all sponsored on behalf of the CIA of the United States government.

A Long and Vile History

The following quote from the late Steve Kangas describes the underlying motivation of just a few of the hundreds of atrocities and crimes committed by the CIA and its predecessor since 1943.

"CIA operations follow the same recurring script. First, American business interests abroad are threatened by a popular or democratically elected leader. The people support their leader because he intends to conduct land reform, strengthen unions, redistribute wealth, nationalize foreign-owned industry, and regulate business to protect workers, consumers and the environment.

So, on behalf of American business, and often with their help, the CIA mobilizes the opposition. First it identifies right-wing groups within the country (usually the military), and offers them a deal: "We'll put you in power if you maintain a favorable business climate for us." The Agency then hires, trains and works with them to overthrow the existing government (usually a democracy). It uses every trick in the book: propaganda, stuffed ballot boxes, purchased elections, extortion, blackmail, sexual intrigue, false stories about opponents in the local media, infiltration and disruption of opposing political parties, kidnapping, beating, torture, intimidation, economic sabotage, death squads and even assassination.

These efforts culminate in a military coup, which installs a right-wing dictator. The CIA trains the dictator's security apparatus to crack down on the traditional enemies of big business, using interrogation, torture and murder. The victims are said to be "communists," but almost always they are just peasants, liberals, moderates, labor union leaders, political opponents and advocates of free speech and democracy. Widespread human rights abuses follow.

This scenario has been repeated so many times that the CIA actually teaches it in a special school, the notorious "School of the Americas." (It opened in Panama but later moved to Fort Benning, Georgia.) Critics have nicknamed it the "School of the Dictators" and "School of the Assassins." Here, the CIA trains Latin American military officers how to conduct coups, including the use of interrogation, torture and murder.

The Association for Responsible Dissent estimated that by 1987, 6 million people had died as a result of CIA covert operations. Former State Department official William Blum correctly calls this an "American Holocaust."

The CIA justifies these actions as part of its war against communism. But most coups do not involve a communist threat. Unlucky nations are targeted for a wide variety of reasons: not only threats to American business interests abroad, but also liberal or even moderate social reforms, political instability, the unwillingness of a leader to carry out Washington's dictates, and declarations of neutrality in the Cold War. Indeed, nothing has infuriated CIA Directors quite like a nation's desire to stay out of the Cold War.

The ironic thing about all this intervention is that it frequently fails to achieve American objectives. Often the newly installed dictator grows comfortable with the security apparatus the CIA has built for him. He becomes an expert at running a police state. And because the dictator knows he cannot be overthrown, he becomes independent and defiant of Washington's will. The CIA then finds it cannot overthrow him, because the police and military are under the dictator's control, afraid to cooperate with American spies for fear of torture and execution.

The only two options for the U.S at this point are impotence or war. Examples of this "boomerang effect" include the Shah of Iran, General Noriega and Saddam Hussein. The boomerang effect also explains why the CIA has proven highly successful at overthrowing democracies, but a wretched failure at overthrowing dictatorships."

"Since 1949 the United States government has been a Dr. Jekyll and Mr. Hyde. On the one hand, the U.S. government was a signatory to the United Nation's Geneva Convention and Declaration of Human Rights. More recently, during the Clinton administration, the government was a signatory to the 1994 Torture Statute. The statute basically said that any US citizen involved in torture outside the United States would be charged with a crime and prosecuted under the statute when they return.

When all of the scandals hit the news media on Abu Ghraib, Guantanamo Bay, and secret torture prisons outside the United States run by the CIA, the graphic pictures of abuse shocked the nation. Many Americans began to see for the first time the clandestine, repulsive side of its government---Mr. Hyde.

George W. Bush and Richard Cheney were not the first politicians to ever pervert American values and the ideals of human rights. Every CIA Director going back to

1947, have kept their dirty little secrets. The uncanny similarity to Nazi Germany during the 1930s and 1940s is unmistakably frightening.

The German people also turned a blind eye and were caught up in the rhetoric of charismatic heads of state and taken in by false propaganda, lies and deceit. Few people remember that the CIA operated a top-secret program called, "Operation Bluebird." It was approved by the CIA Director on April 20, 1950.

This was a behavior modification program jointly undertaken with the Pentagon. Bluebird was a continuation of a Nazi program that had been conducted at Dachau concentration camp. CIA scientists, many of whom were former Nazis, used human guinea pigs at the Pentagon's chemical warfare base in Edgewood, Maryland."

Now move forward in time to the 21st Century. It is now estimated that 100 detainees during the Bush/Cheney years died in custody. Of these, 8 died while being tortured." And, please remember this---there is no Statute of Limitations on murder or manslaughter. So ask yourself this question---why aren't they being tried in a criminal court for these criminal acts?

Society's Inner Conflict over Torture

Ultimately, there are now serious long-lasting value conflicts going on between various segments of American society over the issue of torture. Since things went public, there are those who find torture the epitome of evil incarnate---a violation of human decency, abhorrent criminal behavior that has now put our troops at extreme risk, morally wrong and reprehensible conduct unbecoming of professionals, the likes of which have never been seen before. In effect, it is the perversion of American's highest ethical standards. It is ironic that the very people who are supposed to be protecting our national security are the very ones who are the greatest threat to the American people and, as it turns out, a major threat to the Congress of the United States as well.

They also view a national policy around torture as the promotion of despicable acts not worthy of the highest ideals a people can hold; it dishonors the importance of human rights and dignity, and tarnishes the character of the American people.

There are some in our society today who, reacting under the pressures of terrorist potential attacks, psychologically and morally cave in to these pressures by turning a blind eye to such public disclosures as a national torture policy. Fear and anxiety over potential terrorist attacks dominate and rule these people's beliefs, however unfounded or useless the "ticking Bomb Scenario" might be.

There is still a small percentage of the American public that has no moral qualms where human suffering is concerned, and would give our government a free pass to torture whomever they want.

While the above fearful type may be thought of as pragmatic whose approval of torture is highly conditional (the ticking bomb scenario), the latter group would allow the government to torture anyone they saw fit and exempt government from any control whatsoever. The fearful and anxious group of citizens needs *education*. Those giving government a free pass to conduct torture under any circumstances are not in need of education. Education probably won't help them. What they need most is a *psychiatrist*.

The greatest problem facing both of these latter groups is that they have not taken the time to carefully think things through in any systematic or careful way. One of the key ideas that hasn't been thought through at all by these societal groups is our own system of laws and history of American jurisprudence in the United States.

At the top of the list is the country's century old domestic problem of law enforcement---beating confessions out of detainees (The Third Degree). You will recall Brown versus Mississippi (1936) in which Negro defendants were whipped in order to coerce a confession.

Lynching and murder was the mainstay of a desperate south trying to protect its repressive social order. One-by-one the legal system has slowly purged law enforcement its legacy of violence against the citizenry. When the Rodney King incident occurred in 1991, society was relatively swift to punish law enforcement personnel who engaged in beating Rodney King. But over the decades there have been cases of law enforcement personnel who engaged in other criminal acts such as torture, rape or murder of suspects or jailed individuals without cause.

Or, in the case of police officers committing child abuse or spousal abuse, there is no longer hiding from the consequences of such criminal acts. More recently no one looks the other way or hides their head in the sand when police officers commit unjustified homicides. Just consider all the national and local protests of law enforcement murdering unarmed black men in this country.

And, for those who do bring nothing but shame and dishonor to themselves by such acts, the word *cowardice* does come to mind.

The Problem of the EIT (Enhanced Interrogation Techniques) Timeline

Some politicians (like Dick Cheney) have been suggesting that EIT were responsible for protecting Americans against terrorist attacks on American soil between 2001 and today.

But there is a strange bit of twisted logic in that assumption. Between 2001 and 2009 such CIA tactics as torturing were ostensibly used to acquire intelligence information. The information obtained through torture was then allegedly used to prevent such attacks.

However, enhanced interrogation techniques came to an end in 2009 when President Obama gave an executive order that enhanced interrogation techniques used by the CIA were to be stopped immediately.

But alas here is the rub or distortion of logic. Between 2009 and today there also have been no attacks on American soil. If EIT protected us, why then was the country unharmed between 2009 (six years) and today in the absence of EIT? EIT obviously had nothing to do with why the country has been unharmed during the last 13+ years. Let's be clear: CIA rationalizations around the alleged value of torture are being used to protect those at the highest levels in the government from being prosecuted for **Crimes against Humanity** and quite possibly **Treason.**

Not all Fear of Terrorism is Irrational

Although terrorist attacks have not occurred in the United States since 2001, the fear isn't entirely abnormal or irrational. That is, there have been worldwide several terrorist attacks in Iraq, Afghanistan, Mumbai, India and the Indian Embassy in

Kabul, Bali, Madrid, Paris, London, and a continuous stream of threats from Al-Qaeda against the United States. And, we have a new threat called ISIS. When these events occurred, people became easily manipulated by an exaggerating press.

Add to this the continued fear-mongering by members of the previous Bush administration, there is a rush to judgment as to what ought to be done about terrorist activities here in the United States and worldwide.

Promoting a national torture policy is shortsighted to say the least. Homeland Security's effort to police cargo shipping, ports of entry, airports, aviation schools, and other transportation venues along with security measures to identify all people coming into the country legally and illegally has probably gone a long way toward protecting our country than some clandestine CIA and military program to torture incarcerated detainees.

Dick Cheney in particular wanted the public to be fearful so as to justify, in his mind, the Bush administration's decisions to ignore national laws prohibiting torture, and international laws, including the 1994 Torture Statute and the earlier Geneva Conventions.

Why then is there such a double standard when it comes to torturing foreign military combatants, or prisoners in detention, in places like Guantanamo Bay or Abu Ghraib? Besides fear, anxiety, and an unwillingness to consider the legal, historical, moral, intellectual, humanistic, philosophical, psychological and sociological basis for not adopting policies of torture, there are two other reasons that seem to block the mental ability of some to think things through: (1) An underlying element of ethnic and religious prejudice, bigotry and racism towards detainees or enemy combatants, and (2) lack of foresight into what might be called, "The Opening of Pandora's Box."

In the next section I want to take the reader on a conceptual trip into the Abyss of torture and potential human suffering. This is largely hypothetical but I ask each reader to contemplate what could happen or might have happened if the United States had suffered additional terrorist attacks between 2001 and now.

The Abyss of Pandora's Box

a·byss [ə bíss]
(plural a·byss·es)
n
1. Chasm: a chasm or gorge so deep that its extent is not visible
2. Endless space: something that is immeasurably deep or infinite
3. Terrible situation: a situation of apparently unending awfulness
4. Hell: hell thought of as a bottomless pit

[14th century. Via late Latin abyssus <
Greek abussos "bottomless" < bussos
"bottom"]
Encarta ® World English Dictionary © &
(P) 1998-2005 Microsoft Corporation. All
rights reserved.

One of the reasons for writing this Blog is simply that people I meet just have not thought through this issue with any degree of logic and reason. Just as it took the entire 20th Century to minimize or lessen the use of torture and violence by law enforcement in the United States, it now seems some people want to reverse that trend by starting to compromise where enemy combatants are concerned. It is easy to dismiss such people as being, **"Not Too Bright."**

Unfortunately, things aren't that simple. Those supporting torture are not necessarily stupid (although a psychiatrist might help them). Although reason and logic isn't their strong suit, such people are mostly ordinary, well-meaning people like your neighbor, a family member, or a close friend. This makes their missing the mark all the more befuddling and stupefying. A logical analysis of the torture issue asks a very simple question. That is, where do you draw the line? If 9% of those surveyed give carte blanche to government to torture, then what else lies beyond that line?

If nothing but irrational emotion and value judgments rule the day, then who or what will ever put a limit on buffoons in government from crossing the line to absolute extremism and national insanity?

Consider the following as a hypothetical example of how this might occur.

Let's say this is 2016 and the fear-mongers (mostly conservative republicans and Tea Party members are in control of Washington, and the "loose-cannon media are looking for an exaggeration high to be filled." Let's further hypothesize that three more attacks on American soil have occurred killing an additional 10,000 of our good citizens.

Ultra-conservative politicians want blood and revenge for these attacks and the public is clamoring and demanding action as well. The Vice President gets the assignment. Being overwhelmed and stressed out, he turns to his two confidants, the director of the CIA and the Secretary of Defense. They advise the Vice President to bring in Homeland Security, more senior CIA staff, and the Pentagon to discuss options. They propose to re-institute the 2009 phased-out Enhanced Interrogation Techniques. They want to again torture detainees and re-institute renditions and secret torture prisons overseas.

Always anxious to impress his bosses, a lower level lackey inside the CIA comes up with a proposal that promotes an old concept of graduated responses (like we did in Vietnam) where responses would be in direct relationship to the number of attacks on our soil.

Four levels of response are proposed.

They include a program of **cruelty, brutality, savagery,** and **genocide.** The VP looks at the rest and says, "We once supported a policy of "cruelty" i.e., waterboarding, sexual humiliation, nudity, walling, facial slaps, abdominal slaps, dietary manipulation, wall standing, water dousing, and sleep deprivation. And, at least

8 detainees were murdered by their captors and torturers; well, we've got to do more than that!"

The Vice President then wants to know what else can one do. The lackey tells the VP that the previous program of cruelty was very satisfying and successful. But there is level 2, 3, and 4. The VP inquires, "What are levels 2, 3, and 4?"

The lackey tells the VP level 2 is designated "brutality," "level 3 is savagery," and level 4 is "genocide," where individuals are no longer singled out. Instead this last response is directed toward killing hundreds of thousands, if not millions of people, including non-combatant men, women, and children.

He tells the VP that brutality (level 2) is whipping and beating a detainee to a near-death state, cigarette burning and use of acid on a man or woman's genitalia, and (level 3) savagery involves skinning the detainee, burning flesh with branding irons, convulsive electro-shock, blinding the subject, heating pins/nails and forcing them under fingernails, and of course, cutting off a man's penis and slicing and dicing a women's breasts.

When all else fails to get a detainee to talk, we forcibly hold a detainee's mouth open and force a poisonous snake to enter his or her body (See the Schwarzenegger movie, *Collateral Damage)* for this grisly way to put someone to death. And, like the Nazis following the plot to assassinate Adolf Hitler, hundreds of German officers and government officials, who were alleged to have been part of the plot, were hanged with razor-thin wires making their suffocation and suffering last so much longer.

The VP begins to salivate at these ideas, but he wants to know more about the idea of genocide. The CIA director, with his lackey employee, smile in gleeful anticipation of the answer the lackey will provide.

The VP is told the following:

"Let me give you an example of how this could have worked in our previous war in Afghanistan. We controlled the cities in Afghanistan with troops, sir. What we couldn't control was the countryside and the tribal areas of Afghanistan. (Level 4) is an operational plan to use biological warfare (killing microbes) that could have been used to wipe out everyone in these tribal areas."

"That's fabulous," said the VP.
"But, sir," said the lackey, "that will also kill more than just Taliban, Al-Qaida, or ISIS. It will also kill hundreds of thousands, if not millions, of innocent men, women and children."

"To be honest," said the VP, "we've already committed crimes against humanity with our torture/cruelty program. What is a little more torture, and a little more *Collateral Damage?* **I want all 4 levels implemented right away.**"

This has been just a hypothetical example. However, if push comes to shove and the terrorist attacks were to continue

within the United States, do you really think four levels of response wouldn't be considered by our government?

Let the Generals Speak

October 29, 2008
Retired Generals Condemn Use of Torture

On October 23, 2008, at the University of Virginia Law School retired military leaders Lieutenant General Harry E. Soyster and Lieutenant General Charles Otstott discussed the importance of using interrogation methods that are effective, lawful and humane, and the importance of the commander-in-chief setting the highest standards for all U.S. personnel in the treatment of prisoners.

"It doesn't matter what they do, it's what we do. We don't lower ourselves to the level of this terrible enemy we are fighting. It's about what our standards are."

General Soyster

"The rules are the same, and should be the same. All the Machiavellian work that has been done to get around those rules is detestable, and I can't believe we are doing that as an official policy in the United States of America."

General Otstott

In an article on August 27, 2009, "CIA probe shields architects of US torture regime," its author Bill Van Auken reported on the Obama's administration's cover-up, reluctance to prosecute, and its substantial censorship of the CIA Inspector General's Report on torture.
Given the number of murders that were perpetrated by the CIA, it is flabbergasting that the Obama Administration, which promised "accountability," would fail the American people so miserably in this way.

Bill Van Auken reported that,

"The censoring of information on similar torture deaths means that the Obama administration is acting to ensure that those who planned, ordered, and executed the torture program under Bush are literally allowed to get away with murder.

Nor is this a matter restricted to the three deaths concealed in the report released Monday. Human rights groups have unearthed information on at least 100 detainee deaths during interrogations, and given the cover-ups carried out by the military and the CIA, there is ample reason to believe that there are many more."

An indication of the widespread character of such fatal abuse was given by retired US Army General Barry Richard McCaffrey during an interview on MSNBC television news last April, following President Obama speech to CIA employees at the agency's headquarters in Langley, Virginia.

In that interview General McCaffrey said, "We should never, as a policy, maltreat people under our control, detainees," said

McCaffrey, who made repeated inspection tours of US-occupied Iraq on behalf of the military's Central Command. "We tortured people unmercifully," he added. "We probably **murdered dozens** of them during the course of that, both the Armed Forces and the CIA."

Judgment at Nuremberg Revisited

In 1961 a movie was released called *Judgment at Nuremberg*. The actual Nuremberg trials took place in 1945-46 in Nuremberg, Germany. Although a movie, the final speech by Spencer Tracy spoke volumes to the ramifications of what these trials meant and the long-term impact of crimes against humanity would have on the world.

These trials cut through the rationalizations of citizens following orders of a corrupt and evil dictator. The rationalization, "I was only following orders" carried no weight in the end. Individuals were held responsible for their own acts and were punished or sentenced accordingly. Half of the original 22 defendants were hung.

Current and former members of the CIA, U.S. Army, or higher up political figures will not be allowed to hide from their crimes against humanity by shifting responsibility to "good intentions" or uncertain pragmatic beliefs about results. All that is irrelevant; **what matters is that the United States Justice Department brings criminal offenders to justice and set an example of a democratic country doing what is morally, legally and ethically just.**

As you read ahead, empathetically place yourself inside the mind of Judge Haywood. In the movie Spencer Tracy played Judge Haywood. As you read his words, see the striking connection to what took place this last decade, in particular compared to the

United States at the end of World War II in 1945. One can easily see that society today needs to be reminded of the Nuremberg trials because, indeed, history does seem to repeat itself and governments don't seem to learn from either history or its mistakes. Individuals have memories; institutions do not.

Speech by Judge Haywood Prior to Sentencing

"The trial conducted before this Tribunal began over eight months ago. The record of evidence is more than ten thousand pages long, and final arguments of counsel have been concluded.
Simple murders and atrocities do not constitute the gravamen of the charges in this indictment. Rather, the charge is that of conscious participation in a nationwide, government organized system of cruelty and injustice in violation of every moral and legal principle known to all civilized nations. The Tribunal has carefully studied the record and found therein abundant

evidence to support beyond a reasonable doubt the charges against these defendants. Heir Rolfe, in his very skillful defense, has asserted that there are others who must share the ultimate responsibility for what happened here in Germany. There is truth in this. The real complaining party at the bar in this courtroom is civilization. But the Tribunal does say that the men in the dock are responsible for their actions, men who sat in black robes in judgment on other men, men who took part in the enactment of laws and decrees, the purpose of which was the extermination of humans beings, men who in executive positions actively participated in the enforcement of these laws -- illegal even under German law. The principle of criminal law in every civilized society has this in common: Any person who sways another to commit murder, any person who furnishes the lethal weapon for the purpose of the crime, any person who is an accessory to the crime -- is guilty.

Heir Rolfe further asserts that the defendant, Janning, was an extraordinary jurist and acted in what he thought was the best interest of this country. There is truth in this also. Janning, to be sure, is a tragic figure. We believe he loathed the evil he did. But compassion for the present torture of his soul must not beget forgetfulness of the torture and the death of millions by the Government of which he was a part. Janning's record and his fate illuminate the most shattering truth that has emerged from this trial: If he and all of the other defendants had been degraded perverts, if all of the leaders of the Third Reich had been sadistic monsters and maniacs, then these events would have no more moral significance than an earthquake, or any other natural catastrophe. **But this trial has shown that under a national crisis, ordinary -- even able and extraordinary -- men can delude themselves into the commission of crimes so vast and heinous that they beggar the imagination. No one who has sat at through trial can ever forget them: men sterilized because of political belief; a mockery made of friendship and faith; the murder of children. How easily it can happen.**

There are those in our own country too who today speak of the "protection of country" -- of "survival." A decision must be made in the life of every nation at the very moment when the grasp of the enemy is at its throat. Then, it seems that the only way to survive is to use the means of the enemy, to rest survival upon what is expedient -- to look the other way.

Well, the answer to that is "survival as what?" A country isn't a rock. It's not an extension of one's self. It's what it stands for. It's what it stands for when standing for something is the most difficult!

Before the people of the world, let it now be noted that here, in our decision, this is what we stand for: justice, truth, and the value of a single human being."

Final Comments

The issue of torture and the war crimes committed by members of the government in our name isn't going to go away. The choices are simple. The end does not justify the means and no amount of rationalization is ever going to alter that. No matter how many times someone tries to gloss over it, torture is a **crime against humanity**.

Those who have initiated policies to institutionalize interrogation techniques involving torture, otherwise promoted it, or carried it out, should receive the harshest of punishment, namely death or life in prison. It is not important what position an individual held in our government; those guilty of war crimes need to be brought to justice.

It is an unacceptable act of betrayal and disloyalty to the values of the American people that misguided buffoons in our government led us down the path toward everlasting national dishonor and disgrace.

Given the failure of the United States to follow the principles of international law, and the failure of a sizeable minority of American citizens to comprehend the gravity of a democratic country promoting torture, the "land of the free and the home of the brave" are now in serious moral trouble.

References

Alfred W. McCoy, *A Question of Torture: CIA Interrogation, from the Cold War to the War on Terror,* New York: (Metropolitan Books, Henry Holt and Company, LLC), 2006.

Steve Kangas, Timeline of CIA Atrocities, 1996, online @ http://www.serendipity.li/cia/cia_time.htm available October 9, 2009. The timeline used in Kangas' article is from another source: Primary data source was All history concerning CIA intervention in foreign countries is summarized from William Blum's encyclopedic work, *Killing Hope: U.S. Military and CIA Interventions since World War II*, Monroe, Maine: Common Courage Press, 1995. Sources for domestic CIA operations come from Jonathan Vankin and John Whalen's *The 60 Greatest*

Conspiracies of All Time, Secaucus, N.J.:
Citadel Press, 1997.

Chapter 5

Destruction of the Universal Declaration of Human Rights by the CIA

Introduction

In December 2014 the United States Senate released a long-awaited report on torture by the Central Intelligence Agency (CIA). The report detailed a program of Enhanced Interrogation Techniques (torture) over many years during the post 9-1-1 era by CIA operatives and the U.S. military. The newly released 500-plus-page executive summary of the Senate Intelligence Committee's torture report delivers a scathing critique of the CIA's post-9/11 interrogation programs, revealing previously unknown abuses, media deception, and attempts to avoid Congressional oversight. The summary is based on millions of documents surveyed over five years and is just a fraction of the length of the full, still-classified, 6,000-page report.

This report was very well documented. The CIA did achieve one thing from their actions: No actions of the CIA have been more decimating and abusive than its actions to "piss and defecate" on the Universal Declaration of Human Rights adopted as a Resolution by the United Nations back in 1948.

Background

I am a card-carrying, monetary supporting member of *Amnesty International*. It is the focus of Amnesty International to protect human rights everywhere in the world. Our vision is of a world in which every person – regardless of race, religion, ethnicity, sexual orientation or gender identity – enjoys all of the human rights enshrined in the Universal Declaration of Human Rights (UDHR) and other internationally recognized human rights standards. The UDHR states that "the recognition of the inherent dignity and of the equal and inalienable rights" of all people is "the foundation of freedom, justice and peace in the world."

Universal Declaration of Human Rights

In 1948, the United Nations General Assembly proclaimed the Universal Declaration of Human Rights (UDHR) for all people and all nations. In the UDHR, the United Nations stated in clear and simple terms rights that belong equally to every person. These rights belong to you. Familiarize yourself with them. Help to promote and defend them.

Adopted by UN General Assembly
Resolution 217A (III) of 10 December 1948

WHEREAS recognition of the inherent
dignity and of the equal and inalienable
rights of all members of the human family is
the foundation of freedom, justice and peace
in the world,

WHEREAS disregard and contempt for
human rights have resulted in barbarous acts
which have outraged the conscience of
mankind, and the advent of a world in which
human beings shall enjoy freedom of speech
and belief and freedom from fear and want
has been proclaimed as the highest
aspiration of the common people,

WHEREAS it is essential, if man is not to be

compelled to have recourse, as a last resort, to rebellion against tyranny and oppression, that human rights should be protected by the rule of law,

WHEREAS it is essential to promote the development of friendly relations between nations,

WHEREAS the peoples of the United Nations have in the Charter reaffirmed their faith in fundamental human rights, in the dignity and worth of the human person and in the equal rights of men and women and have determined to promote social progress and better standards of life in larger freedom,

WHEREAS Member States have pledged themselves to achieve, in cooperation with the United Nations, the promotion of universal respect for and observance of human rights and fundamental freedoms,

WHEREAS a common understanding of these rights and freedoms is of the greatest importance for the full realization of this pledge,

Now, therefore, the General Assembly Proclaims

THIS UNIVERSAL DECLARATION OF HUMAN RIGHTS as a common standard of achievement for all peoples and all nations, to the end that every individual and every organ of society, keeping this Declaration constantly in mind, shall strive by teaching and education to promote respect for these rights and freedoms and by progressive measures, national and international, to secure their universal and effective recognition and observance, both among the peoples of Member States themselves and among the peoples of territories under their jurisdiction.

- All human beings are born free and equal in dignity and rights. They are endowed with reason and conscience and should act towards one another in a spirit of brotherhood.
- Everyone is entitled to all the rights and freedoms set forth in this Declaration, without distinction of any kind, such as race, color, sex, language, religion, political or other opinion, national or social origin, property, birth or other status. Furthermore, no distinction shall be made on the basis of the political, jurisdictional or international status of the country or territory to which a person belongs, whether it be independent, trust, non-self-governing or under any other limitation of sovereignty.
- Everyone has the right to life, liberty and security of person.

- No one shall be held in slavery or servitude; slavery and the slave trade shall be prohibited in all their forms.
- **No one shall be subjected to torture or to cruel, inhuman or degrading treatment or punishment.**
- Everyone has the right to recognition everywhere as a person before the law.
- All are equal before the law and are entitled without any discrimination to equal protection of the law. All are entitled to equal protection against any discrimination in violation of the Declaration and against any incitement to such discrimination.
- Everyone has the right to an effective remedy by the competent national tribunals for acts violating the fundamental rights granted him by the constitution or by law.
- **No one shall be subjected to arbitrary arrest, detention or exile.**

- Everyone is entitled in full equality to a fair and public hearing by an independent and impartial tribunal, in the determination of his rights and obligations and of any criminal charge against him.
- Everyone charged with a penal offense has the right to be presumed innocent until proved guilty according to law in a public trial at which he has had all the guarantees necessary for his defense.
- No one shall be held guilty of any penal offense on account of any act or omission which did not constitute a penal offense, under national or international law, at the time it was committed. Nor shall a heavier penalty be imposed than the one that was applicable at the time the penal offense was committed.

- No one shall be subjected to arbitrary interference with his privacy, family, home or correspondence, or to attacks upon his honor and reputation. Everyone has the right to the protection of the law against such interference or attacks.
- Everyone has the right to freedom of movement and residence within the borders of each state.
- Everyone has the right to leave any country, including his own, and to return to his country.
- Everyone has the right to seek and to enjoy in other countries asylum from persecution.
- This right may not be invoked in the case of prosecutions genuinely arising from non-political crimes or from acts contrary to the purposes and principles of the United Nations.
- Everyone has the right to a nationality.

- No one shall be arbitrarily deprived of his nationality nor denied the right to change his nationality.
- Men and women of full age, without any limitation due to race, nationality or religion, have the right to marry and to found a family. They are entitled to equal rights as to marriage, during marriage and at its dissolution.
- Marriage shall be entered into only with the free and full consent of the intending spouses.
- The family is the natural and fundamental group unit of society and is entitled to protection by society and the State.
- Everyone has the right to own property alone as well as in association with others.
- No one shall be arbitrarily deprived of his property.

- Everyone has the right to freedom of thought, conscience and religion; this right includes freedom to change his religion or belief, and freedom, either alone or in community with others and in public or private, to manifest his religion or belief in teaching, practice, worship and observance.
- Everyone has the right to freedom of opinion and expression: this right includes freedom to hold opinions without interference and to seek, receive and impart information and ideas through any media and regardless of frontiers.
- Everyone has the right to freedom of peaceful assembly and association.
- No one may be compelled to belong to an association.
- Everyone has the right to take part in the government of his country, directly

or through freely chosen
representatives.

- Everyone has the right of equal access to public service in his country.
- The will of the people shall be the basis of the authority of government; this shall be expressed in periodic and genuine elections which shall be by universal and equal suffrage and shall be held by secret vote or by equivalent free voting procedures.
- Everyone, as a member of society, has the right to social security and is entitled to realization, through national effort and international co- operation and in accordance with the organization and resources of each State, of the economic, social and cultural rights indispensable for his dignity and the free development of his personality.

- Everyone has the right to work, to free choice of employment, to just and favorable conditions of work and to protection against unemployment.
- Everyone, without any discrimination, has the right to equal pay for equal work.
- Everyone who works has the right to just and favorable remuneration ensuring for himself and his family an existence worthy of human dignity, and supplemented, if necessary, by other means of social protection.
- Everyone has the right to form and to join trade unions for the protection of his interests.
- Everyone has the right to rest and leisure, including reasonable limitation of working hours and periodic holidays with pay.
- Everyone has the right to a standard of living adequate for the health and well-

being of himself and of his family, including food, clothing, and housing and medical care and necessary social services, and the right to security in the event of unemployment, sickness, disability, widowhood, old age or other lack of livelihood in circumstances beyond his control.

- Motherhood and childhood are entitled to special care and assistance. All children, whether born in or out of wedlock, shall enjoy the same social protection.

- Everyone has the right to education. Education shall be free, at least in the elementary and fundamental stages. Elementary education shall be compulsory. Technical and professional education shall be made generally available and higher education shall be equally accessible to all on the basis of merit.

- Education shall be directed to the full development of the human personality and to the strengthening of respect for human rights and fundamental freedoms. It shall promote understanding, tolerance and friendship among all nations, racial or religious groups, and shall further the activities of the United Nations for the maintenance of peace.
- Parents have a prior right to choose the kind of education that shall be given to their children.
- Everyone has the right freely to participate in the cultural life of the community, to enjoy the arts and to share in scientific advancement and its benefits.
- Everyone has the right to the protection of the moral and material interests resulting from any scientific,

literary or artistic production of which he is the author.

- Everyone is entitled to a social and international order in which the rights and freedoms set forth in this Declaration can be fully realized.
- Everyone has duties to the community in which alone the free and full development of his personality is possible.
- In the exercise of his rights and freedoms, everyone shall be subject only to such limitations as are determined by law solely for the purpose of securing due recognition and respect for the rights and freedoms of others and of meeting the just requirements of morality, public order and the general welfare in a democratic society.
- These rights and freedoms may in no case be exercised contrary to the

purposes and principles of the United Nations.

- Nothing in this Declaration may be interpreted as implying for any State, group or person any right to engage in any activity or to perform any act aimed at the destruction of any of the rights and freedoms set forth herein.

Prosecute the Torturers

The following is an article (12/15/2014) that appeared in the online Huffington Post on politics. The article was written by Joe-Marie Burt who is an educator and human rights activist. She teaches at George Mason University and is a Senior Fellow at Washington Office on Latin America. The title of the article is Latin America's Lessons for the US: Prosecute the Torturers.

"The release of the Senate Select Intelligence Committee report on torture has caused great impact, reviving debate worldwide about the United States' use of torture in the aftermath of 9/11. Some have applauded the report, and have noted that torture is prohibited by U.S. and international law and as such those responsible must be held accountable. Those who supported this policy -- including those who put it in motion, such as former Vice President Dick Cheney have decried the report, accusing its authors of bias and reasserting claims that torture kept the United States safe from further terrorist attacks. But they do not deny that torture was used.

As an academic and long-time human rights activist, I welcome the release of the Senate report. Hard-nosed fact-finding and truth-seeking is important in the aftermath of atrocity. A report of this nature can help set the record straight about what happened, and determine, based on careful review of the evidence, whether such atrocities were the doing of a few "bad apples" or of systematic state policy. This is important even when it was long known that the use of torture was official policy during the Bush years.

A report like this can also generate national debate about controversial methods, help citizens evaluate and reevaluate their view of such methods, and determine whether they should be followed by other actions -- including, potentially, criminal prosecutions.

Many of my fellow citizens vehemently repudiate the use of torture, at home or abroad. Over the years I have worked with hundreds of academics, activists, and policymakers who have dedicated their lives to ending torture and other human rights abuses in Latin America and around the world.

Others believe the official discourse repeated ad nauseam during the Bush years that torture -- referred to euphemistically as "enhanced interrogation techniques" -- was both necessary and effective to obtaining key information to prevent future attacks. It is my hope that those who hold this belief will read the Senate report, for if they do they will surely be abhorred by its revelations: that the United States of America, which purports to be a beacon of freedom and liberty, a defender and advocate of human rights, sanctioned the use of torture; and that this is not only a juridical aberration, but a moral one as well.

It is my hope that it will lead them to rethink their views, and repudiate torture and its use forever, here and around the globe.

This leads me to my second point about the Senate report. Its revelations are important on their own, but they also underline the fact that the U.S. government engaged in patently illegal behavior, both by the standard of its own law, and by the standard of international law. The Convention against Torture, which the United States signed and ratified -- and as such is bound by its provisions -- establishes not only the illegality of torture, but also the obligation of states to investigate, prosecute, and punish those responsible for authorizing or committing torture.

The United States stands in blatant violation of its international obligations by failing to move forward on a credible path of criminal prosecutions of those most responsible for the torture program. As such, it undermines its standing in the international arena, and obliterates its credibility as a defender and advocate of human rights around the world.

***

My own research focuses on Latin America, a continent that, when I first began working there, was beset by brutal military dictatorships and fratricidal civil wars. Many of the countries emerging from the dark night of authoritarianism and civil conflict turned to a relatively new practice: the creation of official commissions of inquiry, dubbed truth commissions, that set out to investigate fully the abuses of the past, acknowledge the horrors endured by victims, and make recommendations to provide repair to victims and ensure that such abuses never occur again.

The catchphrase "Nunca mas!" -- "Never again!" -- became the rallying cry of a generation emerging from the dungeons of dictatorship and one of the cornerstones of the modern human rights movement.

Several Latin American countries created official truth commissions to investigate the abuses of past dictatorships. In most cases, still-powerful militaries made fragile new democracies wary of prosecuting human rights violators. When Argentina sought to do just that, convicting first the top generals responsible for the disappearance of thousands of regime opponents, military unrest prompted the government to pass amnesty laws that prohibited further prosecutions. The Uruguayan Congress passed an amnesty law to prevent impending civil prosecutions, citing unrest in Argentina as proof that investigating military abuses would undermine the newly won democracy. In Chile, while a truth commission investigated the Pinochet regime's abuses, prosecutions were not pursued for the same reason. Torturers continued to enjoy their freedom, while victims were robbed of their right to justice for the wrongs committed against them.

Today, years later, many Latin American countries have moved past this situation of impunity for human rights abuses. Amnesty laws have been overturned or ignored, and criminal trials have moved forward in countries such as Argentina, Chile, Uruguay, Peru, and Guatemala.

This has not been a linear or uncontested process--there have been setbacks, as in the quick overturning of the genocide verdict against former Guatemalan dictator Efraín Ríos Montt last year--but the fact is that Latin America is leading the way in demonstrating that it is possible to investigate and prosecute human rights violations.

Some of the most heinous dictators of the region have been tried and convicted --

Videla, Fugimori, Bordaberry, to name a few -- and democracy in those countries is the stronger for it. The Brazilian National Truth Commission -- 50 years after a military coup established one of the longest standing dictatorships in modern Latin American history -- just released its own report, outlining the abuses committed during the military regime and calling for prosecutions of those still-surviving military officers responsible.

Why can the United States not prosecute those responsible for the torture program? The fact is there is no good reason. And if we do not, we run the risk not only of such heinous practices being used again, but of destroying the very democracy we claim to hold so dear. Torture is an affront to human dignity. It cannot be justified, ever. And when it is done in our name, it is our responsibility to act: to stand up, say "Never Again!" and to insist that those responsible be held accountable."

Final Comments

It is important to the integrity of our democracy in the United States that individuals who promoted and carried out torture (Crimes against Humanity) be brought to justice once and for all.

This would include all those within the government, CIA and the military who committed such crimes prior to and during the George W. Bush administration.

Like the Nuremburg trials of post WWII, public trials of former or current government, CIA and military personnel involved in torture needs to be carried out as soon as possible in 2015. Arrest warrants have already been initiated for CIA operatives working in many European countries.

There is no greater duty among those in the United States Congress than to bring to justice all who were perpetrators of Crimes against Humanity. And, it is important to show that the "Red, White, and Blue" has the courage to do the right thing and to admit the mistakes that have been made in our name since 9-1-1. Above all, it must be remembered that there is no Statute of Limitations under federal crimes punishable by death (U.S. Code 18 Section 3281).

To the United States Congress I say this---bring the perpetrators to justice! The integrity of our country can be redeemed if this is done.

Healthcare

Chapter 6
2015

Losing Weight and Getting Into Shape in the New Year
[A Two Part Series]

Part I

Introduction

It won't be long before 2015 is upon us when people tend to make all sorts of resolutions for the New Year. Two popular resolutions are to lose weight and get into shape. Six weeks after the midnight clock turns twelve, most New Year's resolutions are usually forgotten, or people simply give up making the effort.

Part I in this chapter will include: (1) an honest discussion of why a joint simultaneous program of diet and exercise is needed in order to really succeed at losing weight and get into shape, (2) discussion of the aging process and health, (3) self-evaluation and preparation, and (4) dieting basics.

Part II in the next chapter will include: (1) cardio and warm-up exercises, (2) weight-training, (3) flexibility, stretching, and core exercises, (4) cool-down exercises, and (5) supplementation. This will be followed by a summary of the entire program.

As always please see your primary care physician before undertaking such a program. For your health there may be certain foods or exercises that your doctor may find inappropriate for your particular set of medical circumstances or conditions. Once you get the "green light" from your physician, by all means you are welcome to start a program like mine.

Honest Discussion

Most people fail because of a lack of motivation, or because they do not develop a feasible and workable plan. The purpose here is to help my audience develop a feasible and workable plan. This will include combining an effective diet plan along with a very effective cardio, warm-up, weight-training and cool down program.

Combining diet and exercise together is the only sensible approach to achieving the above goals to lose weight and get into shape. It's important not to take short cuts or sidestep difficult moments in any endeavor in life, especially where your health is concerned.

A Word about Motivation

People who become knowledgeable and learn about what's going on in their environment usually develop the proper motivation and the proper skills to succeed in diet and exercise. Knowledge they say "is power." I say usually, but not always.

Knowledge alone is not enough. That is, our defense mechanisms also come into play as well.

One huge defense mechanism that often works against taking action of any kind---is *denial.* Denial occurs most often by creating obstacles that will forgo having to do something. What underlies the creation of such obstacles is rationalization (reasons, however plausible they might appear). In simplest language, people often try to avoid doing difficult things because difficulty implies effort and sometimes sacrifice, and even pain.

Can any blog article, book, or expert make you do something you really don't want to do? Probably not! All experts, personal trainers, doctors, and nutritionists can really do is point you in the right direction. You have to be motivated enough to make the required changes to your life.

To follow my plan will require effort and perseverance. Hopefully I can get you on the right path. But first everyone will need to conduct their own personal assessment. I'll help you with this after the following section.

Everyone can talk about their own personal health in the abstract, but it's really specificity that lures one to take personal action. When I was looking for motivational help, I didn't have to look very far. I started by looking at myself in the mirror. I wasn't a train wreck but certainly was kind of an accident waiting to happen.

Back in November 2013 I joined a gym. I had dieted on and off for many years but this was the turning point for me---combining dieting and exercise to achieve my personal goals; to lose weight, build lean body mass (muscle), and to increase my strength and vitality.

But like all good goal-setting, it needed to be combined with an underlying purpose. That underlying purpose (for me) was to no longer be a Category 1 obese person (in my case 32.5% BMI). I'm 6 feet, three inches tall so, for many years, I was able to hide this obese category 1 from my friends. My underlying purpose was a good reason for shedding the pounds and getting into shape. Old myths about aging die hard. I assumed because I was 70 years old I was "too old" to do bodybuilding. Man, was I wrong! There are men over the ages of 90 (and a few over 100) that compete in bodybuilding contests in the United States and throughout the world.

After one year on my program, I am now at 14-16% BMI and have lost 16 lbs. (which is the result of both gaining lean muscle mass and losing non-essential body fat at the same time). The more muscle you build the easier it is to lose non-essential body fat. I started with a 47 inch waist and now it is 42 inches measured across the belly button; don't measure your waist at the belt line. That type of measurement is two inches below the belly button. If one has got quite a bulge, perhaps one inch above the belly button might be a better way to measure the waist for that individual.

The protective fat that surrounds your bodily organs is known as essential fat---you don't want to lose that fat. My ultimate goal is to be below 10% body fat. As a former social researcher I'm very data-driven in the way I perceive the world and how I come to make decisions in my life. What has influenced me the most is knowledge that being obese increases your chances of getting heart disease, certain types of cancer, stroke, and type 2 Diabetes.

Here are some important statistics (from the Centers for Disease Control and Prevention)[1] regarding the obesity epidemic in this country:

Overview

- More than one-third (34.9% or 78.6 million) of U.S. adults are obese. [Read abstract *Journal of American Medicine (JAMA)*⌐]
- Obesity-related conditions include heart disease, stroke, type 2 diabetes

---

[1] The Centers for Disease Control and Prevention provide a great deal on the information and statistics on Health in the United States.

and certain types of cancer, some of the leading causes of preventable death. The estimated annual medical cost of obesity in the U.S. was $147 billion in 2008 U.S. dollars; the medical costs for people who are obese were $1,429 higher than those of normal weight.

Obesity affects some groups more than others

[Read abstract *Journal of American Medicine (JAMA)*]

- Non-Hispanic blacks have the highest age-adjusted rates of obesity (47.8%) followed by Hispanics (42.5%), non-Hispanic whites (32.6%), and non-Hispanic Asians (10.8%)
- Obesity is higher among middle age adults, 40-59 years old (39.5%) than among younger adults, age 20-39 (30.3%) or adults over 60 or above (35.4%) adults.

Obesity and socioeconomic status

[Read CDC National Center for Health Statistics (NCHS) data brief DF-1.07Mb]

- Among non-Hispanic black and Mexican-American men, those with higher incomes are more likely to have obesity than those with low income.
- Higher income women are less likely to have obesity than low-income women.
- There is no significant relationship between obesity and education among men. Among women, however, there is a trend—those with college degrees are less likely to have obesity compared with less educated women.

The Medical and Social Significance of Obesity

It is important to know that "whether you are seven or 70 lbs. overweight, those extra pounds of fat can spell trouble for your health and your sex life. First, maintaining a healthy weight now will reduce cognitive decline later on.

A study in the March 2009 issue of *Archives of Neurology* investigated whether total and/or regional body fat levels influence cognitive decline. Researchers found that in men, worsening cognitive function correlated with the highest levels of all adiposity measures. The fatter you are, the more likely you will experience cognitive decline later in life."[2]

Another topic related to all this is known as Metabolic Syndrome. According to Dr. Jeffry S. Life, "what's more, your weight affects every aspect of how your body functions. Obesity is such an enormous epidemic that we've created a new name for an old problem: Metabolic Syndrome, also known as Syndrome X. As many as 75 million Americans are now believed to be affected. Simply put, Metabolic Syndrome occurs when excess weight affects your

---

[2] Jeffrey S. Life, The Life Plan, (Atria Books, New York, London, Toronto, Sydney, May 2011 hardcover edition),p.32

health, particularly your heart, as well as your body's ability to process sugar, leading to diabetes.

The five components of Metabolic Syndrome are obesity (especially abdominal obesity), diabetes or insulin resistance, elevated triglyceride levels (one of the fats in the blood), high blood pressure, and increased silent inflammation. There can also be other abnormalities as part of this syndrome, including elevated total cholesterol levels, elevated LDL (the bad cholesterol) levels, low levels of HDL (the good cholesterol), and elevated levels of fibrinogen (a protein that promotes dangerous blood clot formation). Each of these components can also be linked to sexual dysfunction."

The Good News

"Now for the good news---Metabolic Syndrome is completely and totally preventable and reversible. Weight loss, exercise, and correcting hormone deficiencies are the keys to preventing this disease. And, if you already have the syndrome, exercise will also correct the abnormalities that characterize the disease by improving receptor sensitivity. The key is to lose body fat---especially abdominal fat."[3]

The Aging Process and Health

According to Dr. Jeffry S. Life (M.D. and Ph.D.), "We are all going to age, but we don't have to get old. Getting old means the deterioration of health, declining energy levels, loss of sexual function, and loss of your zest for life. I don't want any part of that, and I'll bet you don't either."[4]

Because of the new knowledge that has been generated by research in the last 100+ years, there is now a changing paradigm shift (affecting both the medical community and the individual) in how our medical community thinks about health issues and disease. The traditional way of medicine was to define health as the absence of symptoms or disease. Doctors prescribed

---

[3] Ibid., p.33
[4] Ibid., p.15

medicine and the patient simply played a passive role in his or her own health.

Today that notion of defining health as simply the absence of disease has given way to a new idea that the patient is primarily responsible for his or her own health. Within that idea of responsibility for one's own health is the concept of prevention. And prevention requires a very pro-active approach to prevention of disease and long term deterioration (Use it or lose it!).

The paradigm shift I'm talking about within medicine itself is a shift that includes not only better technology in the treatment of disease, but now recognizes the vast importance of prevention and lifestyle changes. When I was growing up in the 1940s and 50s I was told the doctor was responsible for my health. That is no longer realistic in today's world of health and disease.

Today, all of us need to take responsibility for our own health. What does this mean? Taking responsibility for one's own health means becoming more knowledgeable, taking an active (not passive) role in one's own health care decisions, and maintaining a normal weight, and exercising. Going to the doctor when you are sick just isn't enough; you need to take positive, proactive steps to keep yourself healthy.

Lifestyle changes are the key.

At any age it is imperative that you take inventory of your choices: how/what you eat, how much or how little you exercise, drugs and alcohol, stress, and interpersonal relations. If you haven't thought about these things, you're probably in good company.

But, now the time has arrived for you to go into second gear where your health is concerned. What follows from this point is a workable plan you can use to help you lose weight and get into shape in the New Year. As said earlier, Part I will cover initial preparation and self- evaluation followed by dieting basics. Part II will cover cardio, warm-up exercises, weight training, flexibility, stretching, and core exercises, cool-down exercises and supplementation.

Initial Preparation and Self Evaluation

Besides checking with your doctor as to the advisability of starting a new diet and exercise program, you'll need to do some preparation and a self-evaluation. You can start by taking some initial measurements such as your waist in inches, weight in pounds and your height in inches.

Use a tape measure and measure your waist circumference. Make sure the taped circumference is measured about I inch above the belly button. Why? It is because that measurement is simply more accurate than where one wears a belt, which is usually two inches below the belly button. Many experts think a person's circumference should be 40 inches or less.

However, because 40 inches is a rather arbitrary standard, it won't apply to all people i.e., some people are short, tall, male, female, skinny, fat, young or old. What is needed is a "**Waist to Height Ratio.**"

Although many people use the Body Mass Index (BMI), that measurement doesn't account for the fact that people with very large muscles (muscles also weigh more than fat) are often miscalculated with BMI to be more (because of body weight) fat than people with less lean body mass but lots of visceral fat.

The waist to height ratio (expressed as a decimal) is a simple measurement for assessment of lifestyle risk and being overweight. Compared to just measuring waist circumference, waist to height ratio is equally fair for short and tall persons. This calculation is also valid for children and adults. For example, a man with a 42 inch waist and 75 inches tall would have a ratio of .56 (Overweight).

MEN

- Ratio less than .35: Abnormally Slim to Underweight
- Ratio .35 to .43: Extremely slim
- Ratio .43 to .46: Slender and Healthy
- Ratio .46 to .53: Healthy, Normal, Attractive Weight
- Ratio .54 to .58: Overweight

- Ratio .59 to .63: Extremely Overweight/Obese
- Ratio over .63: Highly Obese

WOMEN

- Ratio less than .35: Abnormally Slim to Underweight
- Ratio .35 - .42: Extremely Slim
- Ratio .43 to .46: Slender and Healthy
- Ratio .47 to .49: Healthy and Attractive
- Ratio .50 to .54: Overweight
- Ratio .55 to .58: Seriously Overweight
- Ratio over .58: Highly Obese

Waist to height ratio 'more accurate than BMI'

Your waist should be no more than half the length of your height, according to experts who claim that having too large a trouser size can dramatically shorten your lifespan.

According to an article written (May 14, 2013) by Nick Collins, Science Correspondent for The Telegraph, United Kingdom:

"Measuring the ratio of someone's waist to their height is a better way of predicting their life expectancy than body mass index (BMI), the method widely used by doctors when judging overall health and risk of disease, researchers said. BMI is calculated as a person's weight in kilograms divided by the square of their height in meters, but a study found that the simpler measurement of waistline against height produced a more accurate prediction of lifespan.

People with the highest waist-to-height ratio, whose waistlines measured 80 per cent of their height, lived 17 years fewer than average. Keeping your waist circumference to less than half of your height can help prevent the onset of conditions like stroke, heart disease and diabetes and add years to life, researchers said. For a 6ft man, this would mean having a waistline smaller than

36in, while a 5ft 4in woman should have a waist size no larger than 32in."[5]

Summary of Preparations

It is essential to follow a healthy diet and to exercise. I recommend to write and record what you eat in a daily food diary (plenty of apps on the computer these days (e.g., Lose It! MyFittnessPal, etc.) Regardless of where you fall on the Waist to Height ratio, a healthy diet and regular exercise is still very important to your personal health and your long-term longevity.

A healthy diet and exercise program can help the skinny man or woman as well as those who are obese. Aging affects everyone, not just the obese.

Dieting Basics

The most important thing about dieting is to keep it simple. Please remember--- calories do count. The first thing you need to know is how many calories you normally

---

[5] Nick Collins, Science Correspondent (UK, The Telegraph), May 14, 2013

consume in a single day. If it exceeds your metabolic rate you are going to gain weight; conversely, if it falls below your metabolic rate you are going to lose weight. It's that simple!

I cannot emphasize enough the importance of keeping a food journal. I know it's tedious but it also is absolutely essential. You'd be surprised how much guessing we all make about how many calories we are consuming. Our errors tend always to be underestimates.

Getting started

Record every calorie you consume for one week. Then divide by seven to derive your average daily intake. This gives you an approximate idea (your actual biological metabolic rate may vary from this average but, for dieting purposes, is close enough) of how many calories you need on a daily basis to maintain your present weight. "Since your goal is to lose weight, you need to decrease this number by 20 percent. Multiply your current daily average by 20 percent, and then subtract this result from your present daily average to get your new daily calorie limit."

In everyone's diet one always needs three basic macronutrients (fats, carbohydrates, and protein) every day (Fat---15%, Carbohydrates---50%, Protein---35%). But how do we derive the right amount of calories for each macronutrient each day? Also, one needs to individualize the calculations.

For example, if your new daily calorie limit is 1800 calories a day, your daily calories for each macronutrient group would be:

Fat (15%)-270 calories

Then, divide this number by nine to convert fat calories into grams of fat. That would be 270/9 or 30 grams of fat per day. For carbohydrates and protein one would divide by four.

Then you need to calculate the number of calories of protein you will need to maximize your muscle-building efforts.

Simply take in 1 gram per pound of your body weight and multiply this number by four (4 calories per gram of protein), and this will give you the number of protein calories you should need each day. If your body weight is 150 lbs. you'll need 150 grams of protein per day. So the number of protein calories you need each day is 600.

Add your protein calories (600) to your fat calories (270) and subtract that number from your new daily calorie limit. In this case, the calculation is 1800 – 870 (270+600) or 930 carbohydrate calories per day. To summarize, based on an 1800 calorie per day diet, the number of calories from fat should be 270, protein 600, and 930 from carbohydrates. For this 150 lb. individual the percentage of daily macronutrients equals:

Fat---15%

Protein---33.3%

Carbohydrates---51.6%

These percentages and the macronutrient calculations will all vary by an individual's own body weight. Two people, with different body weights, on a diet of 1800 calories a day, will each have different percentages of fat, carbohydrate, or protein needed every day.

Now, I have suggestions on *how* to eat and *what* to eat as your diet program. I'll explain the how first then the what.

How to Eat

It is best to eat 5-6 small meals a day. This approach will help stave off that empty feeling many people experience from a diet with just 3 meals a day. Three of my meals are small snacks of no more than 200 calories each in late morning, late afternoon, and late evening. The other three meals are, of course, breakfast, lunch and dinner.

What to Eat (and drink)

When it comes to deciding what to eat, people have very different ideas. What you really need is, first and foremost, a healthy diet. You should stay away, as much as possible, from white breads, white rice, French fries, ice cream, all kinds of sweets, lots of red meat, and all fried foods. Limit your intake of starches, fats, and sugar, and drinking too much alcohol. If something is sold in a can, please be sure to read the label.

I highly recommend each person obtain a master listing of all foods on the glycemic index. What is the glycemic index?

The glycemic index measures how fast and how much a food raises blood glucose levels. Foods with higher index values raise blood sugar more rapidly than foods with lower glycemic index values do.

Explanation:

The body breaks down most carbohydrates from the foods we eat and converts them to a type of sugar called glucose. Glucose is the main source of fuel for our cells. After eating, the time it takes for the body to convert carbohydrates and release glucose into the bloodstream varies, depending on the type of carbohydrate and the food that contains it. Some carbohydrate-containing foods cause the blood glucose level to rise rapidly; others have a more gradual effect. Emphasize using the index to choose fruits and vegetables, beans, grains, lentils, and leaner, better sources of protein.

For almost four years I've been a vegan. However, since starting an intense program of exercise in November 2013, I modified my diet to include good sources of protein such as salmon, eggs, tuna, and soy milk. I needed to increase goods sources of Omega3s as well. But the primary reason for wanting more protein is so that I could build more muscle mass in my body. The more muscle mass the more quickly fat can be burned off.

It is best to use lower glycemic foods in your diet. Once you know what your fat-reducing limit is on the number of calories you should take in daily (2200, 2000, 1800, 1600, etc.). I suggest you prepare your own diet plan based on your own medical situation. I think you should emphasize giving yourself some protein at breakfast, as it will help you feel better throughout the day. Above all, check with your doctor and nutritionist before you launch into dieting. Both the American Diabetes Association and the American Dietetic Association (check out their websites) can also be very helpful in developing diet plans, recipes, etc.

Hydration is important for all of us, but especially when one undertakes a vigorous training program and is dieting as well. "Water is your most important nutrient. You can only live three days without it, and it is involved in every metabolic reaction in your body. Yet most of us don't drink enough liquids during the day. When we are properly hydrated, we feel better, our heart and blood vessels work much better, along with all of our other bodily functions---we think better, our strength and endurance are better, we are healthier, and we live longer."[6]

---

[6] Jeffrey S. Life, The Life Plan, p.64

"If you drink 5 glasses of water per day, a study published in the American Journal of Epidemiology, found that you reduce the chances of a fatal heart attack by 50 percent." Extra water means your metabolism will increase and you will burn more fat. Over the course of a year, if you can increase your water consumption to 1.5 liters a day, you will burn an extra 17, 400 calories, for a weight loss of approximately five pounds."[7]

In Part II ahead I will describe a sound exercise program you can do to meet and exceed your "getting into shape goals" for the New Year. Don't wait; start your planning now.

---

[7] Ibid., p.65

Chapter 7

2015

Losing Weight and Getting Into Shape in the New Year

[A Two Part Series]

Part II

Welcome to Chapter 7, Part II on *"Losing Weight and Getting Into Shape in the New Year."* During Part II, I will cover the exercise component of my program. It will include preliminary information on exercise and losing weight, a sensible cardio program, warm-up exercises, weight training, cool down exercises, and a section on supplementation.

As a reminder I'd highly recommend you obtain your primary care physician's green light before engaging in an intense program of exercise. First, there are a few preliminary things you need to know about exercise and losing weight.

As we all know life is precious. And, living a long life is highly desirable for all of us. With that thought in mind, it is very important that you realize that research may have found "the fountain of youth" after all!

"The One Thing you can do today to live longer---exercise."

"Yes, there's that word again. But as you read, more and more research has emerged showing that exercise lengthens life. Consider just one piece of research: a 2012 study in the journal PLOS Medicine showed that 2.5 hours of moderate exercise per week (that's half an hour of brisk walking a day for 5 days) increased life expectancy by 3.5 years. Those in the study upped their exercise intensity increased life expectancy by 4.2 years. Understand that this wasn't a small group of college students measured over a few weeks. This review looked at data of more than 600,000 people. That's one thing you can do to extend your life. Exercise."[1]

First Things First---Those First Few Weeks of Exercise

Many people have different goals when they start to exercise, such as lose weight, look better, or maintain or improve one's health. Here are some hints to understanding why you should **not** become disappointed at first when you've worked so hard yet that scale of yours doesn't seem to cooperate. You'll come to understand the term *hydration* and its importance. I found an article on the **Spark People** website (in the section Ask the Experts). This question was asked of the experts: *I just started exercising to lose weight, but I've gained weight. Why did this happen?*

---

[1] Jordan D. Metzl, The Exercise Cure, Rodale, 2013, p.2

According to Dean Anderson, Certified Personal Trainer, "When you start doing more exercise, your body begins storing more fuel in your muscle cells, where it can be used easily and quickly to fuel your workouts. The process of converting glucose (carbohydrates) into fuel that your muscles actually store and use (glycogen) requires three molecules of water for every molecule of glucose. As your muscles are building up glycogen stores, your body has to retain extra water for this purpose. That's what causes most of the initial weight gain or lack of weight loss. This is a good thing---not something to worry about.

However, despite what the scale says, you are actually losing fat during this time. The extra water retention will stop once your body has adjusted to the new activity level. At that point, the scale should start moving down. You'll end up with less fat, and muscles that can handle a larger amount."

Realistic Expectations about Building Muscle Mass

The following is an article (posted April 7, 2014) **online** by Wannabebig.com. This article talks about setting realistic goals in your bodybuilding efforts. The essence of the article is that it takes time to build muscle, so please be patient. It may have taken some time to look like you do now, so it will take some time to alter how you look now.

"We all want more muscle, but packing on the weight isn't as easy as just showing up. Find out how much muscle you can gain!"[2]

by <u>Wannabebig.com</u>
Last updated: Apr 07, 2014

"One frequently asked question which always seems to plague gym instructors, Internet message boards, various magazines and books has to do with muscle gain. Many

---

[2] Wannabebig.com, April 7, 2014

of us have heard or have overheard the local gym guru or the community fitness expert boasting about how much he/she has gained, or how one of their clients has gained 10 pounds in a month.

When someone hears this, a light goes on inside their head and it kicks off a series of thoughts that quickly translate into a set of unrealistic goals. I will say this: that from whichever mouth it comes, whether a highly regarded coach, trainer or a bodybuilder, the fact of the matter is that it's physiologically impossible to achieve this muscle status! Later on, I'll explain why."

Making Physical Changes Takes Time

"Often, people making this claim have a faulty perception of how the body either works or are just super-optimistic. Of course, it's not only the gym (freaks) that espouses this myth; it can be traced to numerous ads in a variety of muscle magazines lining the bookstore shelves. The bodybuilding industry, nowadays, thrives on people who are hungry for a quick change.

They are ready to buy into the notion that a change can be accomplished because a certain ad lays claims by way of an incredible cut and paste transformation. Frequently, it's a beginner who testifies to the astounding feat of gaining 30 pounds over a period of several months.

This is, no doubt, a great achievement but most have been fooled into believing that a large percentage is muscle when most of it is due to an increase in glycogen stores, body fat and water.

It's not my intention to dash your hopes or crush your dreams. I'd merely like you to know that the body simply cannot adapt at the speed claimed by many."

For example, Chris Thibaudeau of *Iron Magazine Online* states: "making physical changes takes time." This couldn't be closer to the truth.

"So be forewarned that in your quest to change or morph yourself into the next Ronnie Coleman; the transformation is going to take more than a few months. Our bodies are equipped with systems that need to adapt together over a period. This is what you should bear in mind while working toward the goal of a more muscular physique."

So How Much Muscle Can You Gain?

"Sometimes we are our own worst enemy when it comes to gaining muscle. Nine times out of ten, most of us fail in the dedication department. What starts out as a carefully planned and calculated program, ends up hitting some bumps along the way.

However, even if we are dedicated (some may call it obsessed) and diligent about our nutrition with proper training and recuperation practices, we still would not be able to add more than one pound of muscle in a week. That's right, only one pound per week--and this is assuming you've had a darn good week both inside and outside the gym!"

Hypertrophy

"Hypertrophy is enlargement or overgrowth of a muscle due to the increased size of the constituent cells. Increased training will result in an increase in the size of cells, while the number of cells stays the same.

Often, people believe that if they take in 3,500 more calories during a week that they will be successful at packing on slabs of muscle. However, the old adage that one pound equates to 3,500 calories is right for fat but not muscle. If you want to gain one pound of fat, then you should be taking in an extra 3,500 calories per week. Now there's one way of putting on some weight!

As I mentioned earlier, the body's multiple systems are all intricately interconnected: if one system has not undergone the proper adaptation, then the results will show in the form of a failure to produce optimal hypertrophy of the muscle complex. For example, if we were to look at some of the soft tissues involved in the hypertrophy process of the muscle complex, we'd see that muscle would generally adapt to a load within several days.

Unlike the tendons and ligaments, studies have shown that muscle responds by adapting after a period of several weeks or even months of progressive loading (McDough & Davies, 1984). It also should be noted that the protein turnover rate in collagen occurs approximately every 1000 days.

This clearly shows that even if one were to gain in body weight, the body would only be able to accommodate a certain amount in the form of muscle; otherwise, the muscles would fall prey to injury due to the time span in adaptation rates for various other tissues."

Those who scoff at this and continue to believe they've gained super-size over such a short period forget, as suggested earlier, that much of the increased body weight is largely due to increased body fat stores, glycogen and water."

"IN THE MUSCLES, PROTEIN TURNOVER RATE OCCURS APPROXIMATELY EVERY 180 DAYS (6 MONTHS)."

"Hypertrophy of the muscle complex has, so far, been shown to be controlled by what is known as protein turnover (the breakdown of damaged muscle proteins and creation of new and stronger ones). This process takes time. Just as the many living organisms around us in nature require time to grow, so do our muscles. In our enzymes the protein turnover rate occurs approximately every 7-10 minutes. In the liver and plasma, it's every 10 days. And in the hemoglobin it's every 120 days. In the muscles, protein turnover rate occurs approximately every 180 days (6 months).

This lends even more support to the observation that the turnover rate limits the natural body (of the non-drug-using athlete, bodybuilder) in building muscle quickly.

The Colgan Institute of Nutritional Sciences (located in San Diego, Calif.) run by Dr. Michael Colgan Ph.D., a leading sport nutritionist explains that in his extensive experience, the most muscle gain he or any of his colleagues have recorded over a year was 18 1/4 lbs. Dr. Colgan goes on to state that "because of the limiting rate of turnover in the muscle cells it is impossible to grow more than an ounce of new muscle each day.

In non-complicated, mathematical terms, this would equate to roughly 23 pounds in a year! Keep in mind that high-level athletes are the subjects of these studies."

Putting It All Together

"Now that I've put a damper on your expectations you can step back and take a closer look at your training, nutritional practices and recuperation tactics. There's no need to beat yourself up because you've only been able to gain a pound a week for the last 6 weeks. If anything, assuming your body fat levels has been kept at bay, you're probably on the right track.

When it comes to muscle gain there is no dramatic technique or quick fix that will allow you to pack on more muscle naturally. It's better to stay focused and realistic by training hard, eating meticulously and spending time to recuperate properly; this will result in you achieving a more muscular physique. Keep in mind that it's physiologically impossible to gain more than one pound of lean muscle per week."

"For most weight-gainers, half a pound per week would be an even more realistic goal, because they reach their genetic limit. Remember that gaining muscle is a long-term project and not something that can be simply turned on. If you're dedicated and diligent in your efforts, you'll not be disappointed!"

Proposed Exercise Program for Strength and Fitness

I am proposing an exercise program that will include all the elements of total fitness: Cardio, warm-up exercises, weight training, cool down exercises and supplementation. There are three phases to my program. In Phase I you'll follow my plan for three months. During Phase II my exercise program will be at a more moderate yet advanced level. During Phase III one will be at the most advanced level. By the time one reaches Phase III one should already be physically fit.

Later on you can tweak my program by experimenting with keeping the program more interesting. You don't want to get bored; as you gain more knowledge around the gym (bodybuilding sites on the internet can also assist with knowledge building over time) my program will morph into your program. It is my hope that at the advanced levels (either Phase II or III) you will become hooked on bodybuilding, fitness, and good health. Trying new things is one key to keeping you motivated to continue any health or fitness program.

For the first three months in the gym, I want you to work on building muscle slowly (possibly building just ½ pound of muscle mass per week or, more realistically, only ¼ pound of muscle or 4 ounces per week). After 52 weeks of exercising 3 days a week for 1 hour and 20 minutes your gain in muscle will likely be 4 ounces times 52 weeks or 13.5 lbs. of lean body mass. Combine this with a well-controlled healthy diet and one will look a much trimmer, healthy and better looking person in the mirror.

Do not get worried about what the scale shows as your weight because, at any point in time, it is the sum of you losing visceral fat and gaining lean muscle mass. As the weeks go by one can rest assured if one is looking better in the mirror, your body is definitely losing weight, even if the scale shows only modest weight loss. Combined with Part I's discussion of dieting, I know you can succeed! Before I go any further, here is the recommended sequence of your program in the gym in Phase I, and at the advanced levels (Phase II and Phase III):

Cardio*

Warm-up Stretching Exercises

Weight Training

Cool Down Stretching Exercises

Some people in the gym should probably do some stretching exercises before they jump on a treadmill, stationary or elliptical bike. However, most athletes in the gym using cardio machines warm up by simply starting at a slow speed (usually for 5 minutes). After five minutes your upper body and legs are warmed up. If one is doing cardio outside the gym, I highly recommend one do stretching exercises before they walk jog or run. Limbering up before any exercise is good for preventing injury or unnecessary strain.

Cardio Exercise, Warm-up and Cool down Exercises

Good cardio exercises include walking (slow, medium pace, or power walking), using a treadmill, stationary bike, or elliptical bike. Some people like to jog or run in the outdoors. My preference is to work out in a gym. The most important consideration is how long you exercise rather than the method per se or where you exercise.

"The most important lesson for cardio work is that **you have to stay with it**: Research shows that exercise-induced cardiac protection is lost once regular exercise is stopped. If you stop exercising, the synthesis of those protective proteins comes to a halt. In under a week, you'll be back to your pre-exercise level."

I recommend at least 20-30 minutes of cardio three days per week as a minimum. Others prefer 5 to 7 times per week. However, working out more than 3 days a week can sometimes be counter-productive **if you don't allow enough time for your body to recover** from all your exercise. Actual muscle building occurs during rest & recovery, not necessarily in the gym or outside when you are tearing down muscle fibers.

The sequence I use in the gym is to do 20 minutes of cardio first, and then I do my warm-up stretching exercises (5 exercises should do it) for 5 minutes followed by approximately 45-60 minutes of weight training. After weight training, I do stretching exercises for another 5 minutes (again 5 more exercises should do it).

These stretching exercises are critically important. Your muscles need to be warmed up before jumping into weight training. At the end of weight training, there needs to be a cool-down with stretching exercises. For both warm-up and cool-down exercises, I like to include stretching exercises for the legs, waist (abs and oblique's), and upper body including chest and arms. I work out only 3 days a week at the gym. The days usually are staggered throughout seven days. However, one day at home during my recovery time (as said muscle growth actually occurs on your recovery days where rest and good sleep is necessary) I use a foam roller to improve flexibility in my body. A foam roller is a piece of gym equipment that can be purchased in many sports stores for a reasonable amount of money. Using a foam roller on the floor takes less than 15 minutes of your time. Collectively, all elements of a full body fitness program are covered with my program: strength, balance, flexibility and stamina.

Phase I

Phase I is for beginners. At the beginning of a fitness program you may lack balance, flexibility and physical strength if you haven't been exercising in the months leading up to your decision to join a gym or to undertake a general exercise program.

Phase I is to be followed for three months. If one doesn't feel comfortable going to the advanced program, then feel free to continue working out at the Phase I level until you are ready to move on. One of the first things in Phase I you need to know is what muscles are involved in a good weight training program.

What Muscles Are We Talking About?

When it comes to exercising, what muscle or muscle groups are we talking about?

The following is an overview of the important muscles or muscle groups in the human body. Here is a quick overview of the *Major Muscle Groups*: Legs (Quadriceps and Hamstrings), Glutes, Chest (Pectoralis Major and Pectoralis Minor), Back (Trapezius, Rhomboid, and Latissimus Dorsi), and Shoulders (Deltoid---Anterior, Medial and Posterior).

Here is a quick overview of the *Minor Muscle Groups*: Biceps, Triceps, Abdominals (Abdominal Rectus and Oblique's) and Calves (Gastrocnemius and Soleus). There are many websites available to show you the physiology of muscles in the human body. Much will depend upon how deeply you want to become knowledgeable. This type of detailed knowledge is out there; you just need to seek it out.

Initial Weight Training Program

The following is an overview of the **Major and Minor Muscle Groups** and a sub-listing of exercises one could do (at least 2 sets each as a beginner) as your initial program---primarily directed at beginners although at the advanced level some of these same exercises may apply.

If you do not know what these are specifically, go to any of the bodybuilding sites on the Internet because you'll not only get a written description of these exercises, but also a video of each exercise being performed. This will make learning proper technique and form much easier to absorb. Don't expect perfect execution of technique and form the first time. Like they say, "practice makes perfect." Covering all the major and minor muscle groups will take one approximately 4 workout days to go through one cycle of this beginning program. Then repeat same cycle for 3 months. Good luck!

Major Muscle Groups

Legs

Quadriceps

Leg Press Machine

Hamstrings

Lying Leg Curls

Glutes

Barbell Squats

Close Stance Dumbbell Squats

Wide Stance Dumbbell Squats (between the legs)

Chest

Pectoralis Major

Peck-Deck Machine

Dumbbell Fly's

Dumbbell Press

Low Cable Chest Fly's

Incline: Chest Press (Machine)

Pectoralis Minor

Chest Dips

Barbell Bench Press

Dumbbell Incline Bench Press

Cable Crossover

Back

Trapezius

Reverse Lats Pull Down

Lat Pull Down

Bent Over Two Arm Long Bar Row

Rhomboid

Bent Over One-Arm Long Bar Row

Bent Over Two-Arm Long Bar Row

One Arm Dumbbell Row

Seated One-Arm Cable Pulley Row

Barbell Deadlift

Latissimus Dorsi

Lat Pull Back

Lat Pull Down

Shoulders

Deltoids

Anterior deltoid

Overhead Barbell

Barbell or Dumbbell Upright Row

Incline Barbell Front Raise

Bent-Over Lateral Raise

Reverse Peck-Deck Fly's

Medial   deltoid

Arnold Presses (dumbbell)

Front Arm Raises (cable)

Upright Row (barbell)

Posterior deltoid

Rear Deltoid Lateral (Peck Deck)

Minor Muscle Groups

Biceps

Reverse Grip Rows

Cable Curls

Overhead Cable Curls

Hammer Curls

90 Degree Preacher's Curls

Triceps

Rope Pull Down

Dips

One Arm Cable Triceps Extension

Seated Overhead Dumbbell Exercises

Barbell Shrugs

Seated Curl Push Down

Abdominals

Rectus abdominals + Oblique's

Ab Machine

Oblique Cable Crunch

Bell Tower Crunch

Side Bend with Plate

Standing Oblique Dumbbell

Calves

Gastrocnemius and Soleus

Seated Calf Raises

Standing Calf Raises

Dumbbell Calf Raises

Common Question

One of your first questions upon arrival to a weight training room or facility will be how much weight should I try to lift. As times goes by you'll increase your weights, sets and repetitions (lighter weights---more repetitions; heavier weights---fewer repetitions). However, at the beginning individuals will each have a different answer to this question.

Individuals always vary in their natural abilities. No matter whom you are---start with the lighter weights. You'll have to experiment to get a precise answer. For example, when doing barbell curls should I start with 20 lbs. or 40 lbs.? When I first started to do leg presses I put on only 50 lbs. I found it much too light for my leg muscles. After my first nine months I reached a weight of 405 lbs. doing 5 reps. At one year in the gym I can now do 405 pounds for 20 repetitions (most people in the gym simply call them "reps").

Phase II

The Advanced Program

During Phase I you were exposed to two different ways to exercises your muscles, that is muscles in **isolation** and/or **compound exercises**. An example of muscles in isolation would be to work your biceps or triceps. Compound exercise movements involve several muscles or muscle groups exercised at the same time. While most of the exercises in Phase I are single muscles in isolation, most of the exercises in the advanced program found in Phase II are compound exercise movements with some isolation. **[Please remember to give yourself approximately 1 minute rest time between every set regardless of whether one is in Phase 1, II, or III].**

The most advanced program (Phase III) increases sets and the program's intensity. But it still involves both isolation and compound movements. There is some disagreement in the bodybuilding community in what I'm about to say: **While compound movements are best at developing strength and muscle mass, isolation and the targeting of specific muscles can help to produce better symmetry, tone and definition. Both types of muscle building nevertheless are important and can achieve all of the characteristics above. It all comes down to what your specific goals are i.e., how you want to look. Often these differences are physically reflected among contestants in the *Bodybuilding* versus *Physique* contests.**

You can advance to this more advanced level if and when you are possessed with good strength, vitality, balance and flexibility. What I mean by this is that you are really physically fit.

Phase II

3-Day Compound Movement's

Program with some Isolation

When you are ready to start the advanced Phase II program, try the following:

[5 warm-up exercises]

Day 1(4x8)

Four sets of 8 reps for the following exercises:

Incline Bench Press Barbell

Lat Pull Down

Deadlifts

Shrugs (Dumbbell or Barbell)

Biceps (Bicep curls)

Calves (Use a machine that exercises several muscles on the leg such as calves, hamstrings, and quadriceps at the same time)

[5 cool down exercises]

[5 warm-up exercises]

Day 2 (5x5)

Five sets of 5 reps for the following exercises:

Incline Bench Press---Dumbbell

Bent over Rows

Squats

Upright Barbell Rows

Triceps (Rope pull down)

Abs (Ab Machine)

[5 cool down exercises]

[5 Warm-up exercises]

Five sets of 5 reps for each of the following exercises:

Day 3 (5x5)

Incline or Decline Hammer

Cable Rows

Romanian Deadlift

Military Seated Press (or standing)

Abs (Bell Tower)

[5 cool down exercises]

Phase III

At about one year into my training program one should be ready for my most advanced level (Phase III). I want to make it clear that after Day 2 one might want to experiment with the Day 3 program. In my case I wanted to do more isolation muscle training involving my biceps. Someone else might need to work toward better symmetry with their calves, chest or back muscles.

You'll know by then which way to go. For now here is my advanced Phase III program:

Phase III Advanced Bodybuilding Program

Primarily Compound Movements

There are a total of 415 reps in this 3 day program

Day 1

[5 Warm-up exercises]

Flat Bench Press   4 sets of 8 reps

Squats   4 sets of 8 reps

Deadlifts   4 sets of 8 reps

Clean and Press   4 sets of 8 reps

[5 Cool-down exercises]

Day 2

[5 Warm-up exercises]

Military Press   4 sets of 8 reps

Bent Over Rows   4 sets of 8 reps

Upright Rows   4 sets of 8 reps

[5 Cool-down exercises]

Day 3

[5 Warm-up exercises]   Additional
Isolation Exercises

Five Best Bicep Exercises

Barbell Curl   4 sets of 8 reps

Incline Dumbbell Curl   4 sets of 8 reps

Standing Biceps Cable Curl   4 sets
of 8 reps

Reverse Grip Bent-Over Rows   4 sets
of 8 reps

Concentration Curls   4 sets
of 8 reps

[5 Cool-down exercises]

Supplementation

The last part of this program involves supplementation. This can sometimes be a "touchy subject" for health and safety reasons, and for reasons related to alleged effectiveness and additional cost.

Most people are aware of the dangers of steroids and bodybuilding. There are lots of supplements being advertised that are supposed to help you as an athlete, no matter what sport or activity one is involved with. My strongest recommendation is first see if you have any deficiencies. My deficiencies turned out to be iron and vitamin D3. I took steps to remedy the situation. Once you address the issue of deficiencies, some supplements may be very helpful to supporting your body's ability to handle a vigorous exercise program.

I recommend the following supplements based on recommendations in Dr. Life's Plan:

- A multivitamin and mineral supplement daily
- Getting enough fatty acids in the proper amounts (Omega 3, 6 and 9)
- A probiotic supplement
- Vitamin D3
- CoQ10
- Saw palmetto
- Lycopene
- Milk thistle
- Calcium
- Pycnogenol/L-arginine [3]

First however, discuss any and all supplements you currently take, and those you are planning to take, with your primary care physician. There may be reasons in your particular medical profile that requires you **not** take certain supplements. This might be due to possible adverse reactions with any medicines you are already taking.

---

[3] Ibid., p. 297-298

Individuals have different medical needs; therefore, what you take in supplements must be done cautiously. That said, I do recommend some supplements for good health and as a kind of insurance policy, but also to aid your body during an intense exercise program.

Summary

There are no guarantees in life. If you don't eat right and exercise there is also no guarantee of a long life. What I've offered is a simple road map to meeting any New Year's resolutions you may have that involve dieting and getting into shape. Many people have good intentions but never follow through. But this will be your year to succeed. As they say, "better late than never." Good luck!

Chapter 8

The Coming Revolution in Bodybuilding

Maximum Contraction Training

[The Science behind How Muscles Get Larger]

Introduction

Today there is a revolution going on in bodybuilding. It isn't always visible, but it is there nonetheless. People have assumed for many decades that building muscle successfully required one to be in the gym 6 days a week with 2-3 hour workouts. That assumption is no longer the case.

What revolution am I talking about? It is a revolution that propels all of us in the bodybuilding world to consider and take note of a more "science-based" approach to bodybuilding. Why? Because for decades opinions among bodybuilders, trainers, and others have varied so much (often without any scientific basis at all) as to the **best way(s)** for one to develop and achieve a ripped, lean and mean bodybuilding machine, a physique and healthy body one can be proud of.

These ideas that follow apply to both men and women. Our whole concept of how to achieve the best bodybuilding results has been turned up-side-down and on its head. To make things clear I will do several things:

- I will provide an overview of Maximum Contraction Training, its origin and its principles
- I will discuss how muscle fibers actually work to maximally increase muscle strength and size
- I will provide a sample program one can use that effectively builds muscle

in less time, and with greater results. In addition, I will discuss how often one should workout and the role that rest and recovery time plays in developing greater strength and muscle size.

- Finally, I will discuss my own experience that will demonstrate that Maximum Contraction Training really does work, even for an older bodybuilder like me (age 72).

Overview of Maximum Contraction Training

Two important people contributed to the principles and refinement of Maximum Contraction Training. They are John Little (Max Contraction Training---*The Scientifically Proven Program for Building Muscle Mass in Minimum Time, [Contemporary Books, McGraw Hill Companies, 2004]*) and Mike Mentzer, ([with John Little] *High-Intensity Training the Mike Mentzer Way, McGraw Hill, 2003*).

So what is Maximum Contraction Training?

"Maximum Contraction Training is based on one simple premise: there is one position in any muscle's range of motion that is more productive than any other. This one position involves a muscle's greatest amount of fibers---and when sufficient resistance is applied to a muscle when it's in this position, more muscle fibers will be recruited and stimulated to grow bigger and stronger. Using a training approach that follows this premise will produce results many times greater than the growth stimulation imparted by conventional bodybuilding protocols, such as lifting a weight up and down."[1]

One of the things to realize in Maximum Contraction Training is that intensity, not

---

[1] John Little, Max Contraction Training, , p. xii

duration is the key point in understanding how one can get stronger and get better, quicker results.

"There are a host of ancillary benefits that attend training with Maximum Contraction apart from its power to dramatically increase muscle size and strength, including a reduction in body fat levels, stress release, and a huge savings in the time required to realize all of the above."[2]

John Little went on to write that, "Ever since the public became seriously interested in bodybuilding during the fitness boom of the 1980s, hundreds of theories have been advanced on how best to proceed with the prospect of growing bigger and stronger muscles. Unfortunately, almost all of these approaches made the cardinal error of assuming that muscle building and strength

---

[2] Ibid. p. xiii

training must be performed with an eye toward conditioning the body to tolerate longer and longer exercise sessions. However, science has revealed that it is not the duration but the intensity of the exercise that is solely responsible for effecting an increase in muscle size and strength and, hence, personal appearance. (Muscle is what gives both sexes their desirable shape, fat being formless.) Intensity and duration exist in an inverse ratio to each other; thus, the higher the intensity, the briefer the workout must be."[3]

In a nutshell, here are the critical conclusions drawn by John Little's 20+ years of consulting exercise scientists and champion bodybuilders in developing an effective and scientifically sound bodybuilding program like **Maximum Contraction Training:**

---

[3] Ibid. p. xii

- That only one set lasting a mere 1 to 6 seconds is required to effect increases in muscle size and strength (i.e., you do not need multiple sets of an exercises for any given body part).
- That this same 1-6 second time of contraction (TOC) is more important than repetitions.
- That movement through a full range motion is less valuable for size and strength increases than is a full or maximum contraction that is for the TOC indicated.
- That only two workouts per week are required to make optimal (not minimal) progress---and even *less* training is required as you become bigger and stronger.
- That an increase in lean body tissue will result in a substantial raise in your basal metabolism rate, allowing you to burn more calories at rest and lose more fat, thereby negating the need for

deprivation dieting and hours of aerobic exercise each week.

- That a well-balanced diet will provide all the nutrition your body requires to allow you to lose fat, build muscle, and have more energy (i.e., you do not need supplements; supplements have been over-emphasized for commercial reasons and do nothing to stimulate muscle growth, nor will they allow the body to build muscle or strength faster).

- That a productive workout requires no more than 1 minute (maximum) and 10 seconds (minimum) of total training time to complete.

- That you can improve "problem" body-parts and build impressive levels of muscle size and strength on virtually any type of progressive resistance equipment (from machines to free weights)---if you correctly employ this new protocol and its principles.

- That you need only perform a 1-second maximum contraction once every two weeks to maintain the gains you make on this new system.
- That you do not need to spend hours a day and multiple days per week in the gym to build a muscular body and to dramatically increase the size and strength of your muscles.[4]

How Muscle Fibers Grow

While muscle strength and muscle mass do not have a direct one-to-one relationship, there is definitely a connection between the two. To understand exactly what that connection is and how big a role it plays, it helps to have a little background on the fundamentals of muscle physiology. This topic can get very detailed and complex, so I've opted to provide my cyber audience with a less

---

[4] Ibid. p. xiii

complicated, less detailed description of muscle fibers and how they work.

Muscles are composed of connected bundles of **muscle fibers**, of which there are two kinds: slow-twitch and fast-twitch. **Slow-twitch fibers** are considered the endurance fibers, because they are very resistant to fatigue but cannot contract as quickly or as strong as their counterpart.

Fast-twitch fibers are considered the strength or power fibers because they fatigue quickly but have explosive speed and power. Most muscles are a mix of both slow and fast-twitch fibers (which in turn are made up of protein bundles called **myofibrils**).

The exact mixture of slow/fast is for the most part fixed at birth and varies depending on numerous factors including the muscle type and genetics. To make it clear how these types of fibers react during weightlifting, consider the following example from John Little's book, Max Contraction Training :

"In conventional training methods, one performs repetitions or a series of contractions. A typical set of repetitions sees one initiate a given movement in a position of literally zero resistance. Then, as the weight is moved, the muscle shortens or contracts until it finally ascends to the position of full or maximal contraction. In this final position the greatest number of muscle fibers are brought into play and stimulated to grow bigger and stronger. And yet the conventional protocols, this position of Maximum Contraction is seldom, if ever emphasized, with the result that maximal growth stimulation is seldom, if ever, achieved. A perfect example of this is the leg extension exercise performed in the conventional manner (i.e., up and down). Looked at physiologically, this exercise will see the trainee initiate the movement using only the barest amount of muscle fibers required to do the job. At the halfway point, a few more muscle fibers will have been called into play and then, at the position of full muscular contraction or where the legs are fully extended, as many fibers as can possibly be recruited will be activated to keep the resistance in this fully contracted position. However, long before the fibers have been stressed maximally, the resistance is typically lowered (often dropped), giving the momentary stressed quadriceps muscles a chance to disengage (and recover to a certain extent), which is the very opposite effect of what you should be trying to accomplish."[5]

John goes on to explain more on the timeframe for this type of muscle action:

"This means, in effect, that in a given 10-rep set which lasts about 60 seconds, maximum muscular involvement takes place for a total of only 10 seconds---only 1 second after every 5. So out of a possible 60 seconds' worth of maximum muscle stimulation, the trainee is obtaining only 1/10 of the results he is capable of deriving from the movement. Viewed in this light, it

---

[5] Ibid. p.94

becomes painfully obvious that the trainee is wasting the other 9/10 of the time he's been employing on the exercise. Conversely, when a given muscle group is brought into a fully contracted position and made to contract maximally against a heavy resistance for a full sixty seconds, the maximum amount of muscle fibers that can be activated to assist in the task will be called into play and thoroughly stimulated until they are incapable of supporting the full contraction. As soon as the trainee can no longer hold the contraction, he will have effectively exhausted all of the muscle fibers involved in that contraction, that is, all of them."[6]

Sample Max Training Program

In order to keep this blog a reasonable length, I suggest you learn the details of the following exercises, and the muscle or muscle groups involved, from other sources

---

[6] Ibid. p. 94-95

at your leisure. Reading John Little's and Mike Mentzer's book mentioned above is a good starting point. Another good source is simply the Internet.

Selecting the best possible set of exercises is very important. Not all exercises lend themselves easily to Maximum Contraction Training. "Certain exercises performed with conventional equipment don't incorporate the proper physics to provide maximum resistance in the fully contracted position. I'm thinking here of movements such as squats, standing barbell curls, and most types of pressing movements wherein the resistance falls off once you're past the halfway point of the movement. It is this lack of resistance in the fully contracted position that makes these exercises inefficient for Maximum Contraction Training. Exercises must be selected that enable a targeted muscle group to be moved into a position of full muscular contraction against resistance and held there for 1 to 6 seconds. Experience has revealed the following exercises to be perfect for Max Contraction Training, as they fulfill the criteria just described and, thus, allow for maximum muscle growth stimulation:

Exercise
Muscle Group

1. Leg Extensions
   Quadriceps
2. Leg Curls
   Hamstrings
3. Standing Calf Raises
   Gastrocnemius
4. Max Straps Pulldowns
   Latissimus Dorsi
5. Shrugs
   Trapezius
6. Pec Deck
   Pectorals
7. Lateral Raises---Side and Rear
   Deltoids
8. Bent-over Laterals
   Rear Deltoids

9. Max Straps Kickbacks
   Triceps

10.   Palms-under, Close-Grip

       Chins or Steep-Angle

       Preacher Curls
Biceps

11.   Max Straps Crunches
       Abdominals"[7]

Workouts---How Often?

The answer to this can be highly individualistic because people of different ages, weight, gender, experience and fitness level---would all differ.
Also, it is very important to point out that the amount of recovery and rest needed also may differ. However, here are some tips or key points to remember:

---

[7] Ibid. p. 103

- Beginners should work out no more than three times per week; intermediates should train only twice a week; and advanced trainees should limit their training to only once a week.
- Beginners may sustain their Maximum Contractions for up to 60 seconds; intermediates and advanced trainees should increase their resistance and aim for 1 to 6 seconds.
- Train your whole body each session.
- Never perform more than 12 sets in any given workout. (Intermediates should perform only 10 total sets in any given workout).
- When specializing, beginners should perform only 5 sets for the body part being specialized on, with each set being a legitimate all-out effort. Intermediates should reduce their sets for the targeted muscle group to a maximum of 3.

- Work the specialized body part first in the workout (when your energy levels are highest) and then your other body parts in descending order (i.e., from the largest to the smallest).
- Take one full week off from weight training every 10 weeks.
- When not specializing, select a different body part every month. This ensures balanced development and prevents overtraining of any one muscle group.[8]

My Own Experience

I decided in November 2013 to join a gym with my wife. I was a kidney cancer survivor. I was also at that time a 70 year old Type II diabetic (diagnosed in 1991), overweight sedentary person with high blood pressure. Consequently, I was long

---

[8] Ibid., p. 114

overdue to get my act together and dramatically change my lifestyle.

The decision to get serious about getting into shape was one of the *best* decisions of my life; I have never looked back.

At that time I started working out three days a week doing 35 minutes cardio, along with additionally spending 1 hour, 10 minutes in the weight room each workout session. I chose the stationary bike to do my cardio, and began a full body workout (8 machines and a few free-weights at first). During that first year I fine-tuned my weight room program that included more free-weights. I made a transition to include more compound exercises (e.g., bench press, deadlifts, squats, leg presses, leg extensions etc.). In the weight room I soon added 5 warm-up and 5 cool-down exercises to my program. I studied all the time to improve my program.

Results for Year 1

During that first year I lost 23 lbs., took 6 inches off my waistline (from 47 ½ inches down to 41 ½ inches) and my chest size increased from (45 inches up to 49 inches). My neck size decreased from 18 inches down to 17 ½ inches. I also went from a 32.5% BMI (Body Mass Index) down to a comfortable 14-16% BMI.

People noticed my physical changes and were very complimentary. Ten reps per exercise and 2 sets each was my typical effort. And, in general, I did 15 different weight room exercises per workout altogether, not including my 5 warm-ups and 5 cool down exercises.

My psychological self-esteem increased and I was becoming more confident with every workout session as I continued to improve. But, while some experts may disagree with what I'm about to say, I believe that the greatest mark or indicator of fitness is **Physical Strength.** However, it really depends on your goal. If your goal is to build muscle size and strength, then strength is really your measure of fitness. If your goal is to run 26 miles in a long distance race, then endurance is your fitness measure. Sprinters have large muscular bodies (the mesomorph look) due to the high intensity, and activation during training, of fast twitch muscle fibers. Conversely, long distance runners tend to have smaller leg muscles, thinner bodies (the ectomorph look) due to greater use of slow twitch muscle fibers.

If your goal in later life is to ward off the ravages of frailty, then give greater priority to weight training and muscle development. It turns out that weight training gives you both a good cardio workout at the same time as one lifts weights for muscle mass. Emphasizing cardio alone does only one thing; weight training however does both.

With every exercise added during that first year, I increased my ability to add more and more weight or additional reps almost all the time. For example, I started out with only **45 lbs.** doing 10 reps for chest exercises. In a few months I was able to increase that weight to **100 lbs.**

It's an individual thing but I found out over the months that my leg and back muscles were getting really strong. On the calf machine I started with **100 lbs.** and worked my way up to **150 lbs.** doing 2 sets of 10 reps.

I started out at the beginning on the back machine doing 10 reps of **90 lbs.;** long before the end of the first year I was pulling down 8-10 reps of **245 lbs.**

Enter 2015 and Maximum Contraction Training

My good progress during my first year in the gym was due, I think now, to the fact that I constantly was adding more and more resistance to every exercise. However, I was still doing lots of reps, not using maximum weight resistance, nor holding the weight 1-6 seconds. But in 2015 all that changed.

In January 2015, I started a new program of **Maximum Contraction Training.** I thought of this program initially as experimental because, like many of my fellow bodybuilders and trainers, I was still locked into the conventional way of thinking about exercise and the notion that I had to stay in the gym as long as possible in order to maximize or achieve good results.

The length of time required to do my cardio remained the same; however, in the weight room I'm now going through 9-10 exercises (I consider myself an intermediate) in less than 45 minutes which includes set-up time, in addition to the time I exercise with high intensity for each exercise. What I achieved in my first year (using conventional bodybuilding approaches) in terms of physical strength increased dramatically in as short a period as 10 weeks. **The following are some of the highlights of this effort:**

While I started the New Year utilizing 120 lbs. on the Peck Deck (chest) machine, I'm now able to hold 200 lbs. at maximum contraction for 30 seconds. In order to use enough resistance, so I can only hold the weight for 1-6 seconds, I will have to increase the weights on this machine somewhere well north of 200 lbs.

I can now leg press 1,060 lbs. for 6 seconds. I now can do a traditional deadlift of 225 lbs. and can do a stronger-range deadlift of 270 lbs. My leg extensions went from 60 lbs. to 250 lbs. My leg curls went from 40 lbs. to 210 lbs. I won't bore you with the rest.

So the question remains, besides strength did I achieve in 10 weeks better bodybuilding measurements with Maximum Contraction Training?

The answer is a resounding "Yes."
Here is the data:

Initially in November 2013 I had 16" biceps. And, in that first year it was reduced in size to 15 ¼" because fat covered the muscles. I took my measurements at the beginning of Maximum Contraction Training. Here are the results after 10 weeks:

<u>Beginning</u>		<u>after 10 weeks</u>
Neck	17 ¾ inches	17 ¾ inches
Biceps	15 ¼ inches	15 ½ inches
Chest	49 inches	49 ½ inches
Waist	41 ½ inches	41 inches
Quads	22 ¾ inches	23 inches

Post Script

My improvement in bodybuilding measurements indicated that I (increased or decreased) in the right direction ¼ inch to ½ inch on 4 out of 5 measurements. You may not think this is an extraordinary improvement--- until you realize these results were obtained in only 10 weeks by a 72-year old bodybuilder.

Needless to say I am very happy with the results and am now continuing to exclusively use the exercise protocols of Maximum Contraction Training. I expect this new revolution in bodybuilding to continue. Maximum Contraction Training is scientifically sound and simply too good to pass up.

Religion

Chapter 9

The Truth Value and Interpretation of the Holy Bible

It is between fifty and sixty years since I read [The Apocalypse] and I then considered it merely the ravings of a maniac, no more worthy or capable of explanation than the incoherence of our own nightly dreams.

Thomas Jefferson (Third President of the United States, 1743-1826)

Background

This chapter is a modified excerpt from a book I wrote between 2005 and 2009, "titled---*Trouble in Paradise: The Decline of Christianity in the 21st Century.* For those of you who haven't read this book, this chapter should provide information and facts that are central to the following question: **How was the Holy Bible really created?**

There are two ways people generally view the Holy Bible: (1) as the "Received View" based on faith, and (2) as the "Historical View" based on valid historical facts. True Christian believers tend to follow the Received View, while academics and religious scholars tend to support and accept the historical view. Both viewpoints attempt to see "Truth" as supporting their viewpoint. For the true believer facts are irrelevant, only faith and belief matters. For the academic or scholar, facts and data are the only things that matter. This conflicting difference between the two viewpoints automatically begs the question---what is truth?

What is Truth?

So what is truth anyway? Is my truth the same as your truth? Is truth absolute or is it variable, conditional, a product of culture, or depend entirely upon the interpretation of the word itself? Is truth only a matter of faith or are there empirical ways of getting at the truth? Well, it appears that truth is not absolute. Truth is, quite simply, what we agree it is (no more and no less). It is a matter of consensus that can change over time. Scientific truth operates in this conditional sense of everything being subject to change. So, why not any other "type" of truth?

Theologians, when discussing truth, would answer that everything has a cause and that cause is God. In their opening pages to their book, *The Idiot's Guide to the Bible,* the authors ask a thought provoking question in their own right. If everything has a cause (as theologians assert) then what caused God? Theologians, of course, don't answer that question and can't answer the question.

At one level these questions are asking for an answer that is logical, empirical and straightforward, based on reason and facts. Most of us lead lives that are rather pragmatic and ordinary where we tend to answer everyday questions using facts and reason. At another level some questions simply have an underlying dimension of value judgments. The *answers* to these value-laden, judgmental-type questions also tend to be *value-laden, judgmental-type* answers.

Answers are not facts or data but statements of value instead. For example, people on both sides of the abortion issue often ask and answer questions that are riddled with value judgments. Another example of a value judgment question (*it must be remembered that many cherished beliefs are really cherished values*) is–what is the purpose and meaning of one's life? Since everyone presumably would have a different purpose in life, this question is really asking, "Does my life have value?" Science, of course, is unable to answer judgmental or value-laden questions such as meaning and purpose, including the ultimate value of one's life. Theologians and ministers ask these types of value-laden questions and provide value-laden answers every day.

At times it is true that scientists also make value judgment statements about the value of research findings, and the delight and joy at making discoveries and unraveling the laws of the universe. People will mostly agree that there is value when science does succeed when cures are found for illness and new medicines are created in the laboratory.

However, that is where the similarity between science and religion ends. Knowledge and methodology separate physical science, medicine, and the social sciences from religion. While the physical sciences (chemistry, biology, physics and medicine) came on strong from the 17th century on, the social sciences of psychology and sociology made their strong entry and debut into the world of science, and scientific methods, during the 19th and 20th centuries.

Knowledge in medicine and the physical and social sciences are contained in books, articles, and academic journals. Such a body of knowledge goes back in time regarding the content of the material. In addition there are over 1500 formal academic journals published around the world each month. Each journal usually covers 10-12 articles on new research findings that have passed muster by a professional peer-review process.

Unlike the quality and quantity of authoritative serious knowledge created and reported upon by scientists today, religions rely almost exclusively on ancient documentation to support their belief systems.

In order to provide religious answers on meaning and purpose, special documentation was needed. In Judaism, it is the Old Testament accepted as the Hebrew bible. In Christianity it is the Hebrew bible and the New Testament. In Islam it is the Koran. Scriptures are used to teach adherents and to serve as justification for a particular belief system.

This is only speculation, but perhaps the first writers of the Judaic and Christian gospels needed to "market" the material as– you guessed it–*"**The Word of God.**"* If God is the real author and architect of the Bible, He would be much better than some nondescript followers of Jesus. Ever wonder why there is so much debate as to who wrote this chapter or that chapter in the Bible?

One must remember that in the timeline for authorship in the Old Testament their mythological stories were created by men centuries before the New Testament. In order to garner support for the New Testament, someone among Jesus' later adherents to the new religion came up with the bright idea that wouldn't it be nice to hijack the scriptures of another religion and call it their own. If Judaism's Old Testament were borrowed, wouldn't that increase the probability that other non-Christian Jews might throw their support to the fledging Christian religion?

Interpretation of Scriptures

In Christianity one problem that surfaces is that the documentation provided is itself highly problematic and questionable as a source of any kind of authority in its own right. In the case of the 27 books of the New Testament and 39 books of the Old Testament, interpretation of scriptures is not a straightforward process. Far from it! Differences of opinion are everywhere from biblical experts, scholars, and from biblical archaeologists on the one hand, to practicing priests, ministers, and Christian schools on the other. In fact, even among believers there is great diversity of opinion as to whether scriptures hold any "truth value" for them.

One important reason scriptural interpretation is so varied is that the Bible itself is believed to have had many authors and many scribes to convey its content. Richard Dawkins has commented that, "The fact that something is written down is persuasive to people not used to asking questions like: 'who wrote it, and when?' 'How did they know what to write?' 'Did they, in their time, really mean what we, in our time, understand them to be saying?' 'Were they unbiased observers, or did they have an agenda that colored their writing?'

Ever since the nineteenth century, scholarly theologians have made an overwhelming case that the gospels are not reliable accounts of what happened in the history of the real world. All were written long after the death of Jesus, and also after the epistles of Paul, which mention almost none of the alleged facts of Jesus' life. All were then copied and re-copied, through many Chinese Whispers generations by fallible scribes who, in any case, had their own religious agendas."

If one thinks that these differences are occurring only in the modern era, he or she is poorly informed. Before the orthodox only abbreviated viewpoint of Christian literature was assembled into what we call the Bible today, the rich tapestry of comprehensive writings on Christianity from many different sources were, for the most part, circulating throughout the ancient religious communities of the Middle East.

Diversity of Opinion in Early Christianity

There was no New Testament for early Christians. The books that were eventually collected into the New Testament had been written by the 2nd century but had not been gathered yet into a widely recognized and authoritative canon of Scripture. The best way to determine if early Christians held differing opinions about Christ and Christianity is to know what their beliefs were and how they differed.

For example, according to Erdman, "The wide diversity of early Christianity may be seen above all in the theological beliefs embraced by people who understood them to be followers of Jesus." Erdman goes on to cite an impressive offering of different beliefs among early Christians of the second and third centuries. Among those Christians, some thought there was just one god, and others believed there were two gods. Some thought there were thirty and some even believed there were 365.

There were Christians that thought God created the world; other Christians thought or believed that this world had been created by a subordinate, ignorant divinity. (Why else would the world be filled with such misery and hardship?). Yet other Christians thought it was worse than that, that this world was a cosmic mistake created by a malevolent divinity as a place of imprisonment, to trap humans and subject them to pain and suffering.

There were Christians in the second and third centuries who believed that the Jewish Scriptures (the Christian "Old Testament") was inspired by the one true God. Others believed it was inspired by the God of the Jews, who was not the one true God. Others believed it was inspired by an evil deity. Others believed it was not inspired.

"In the second and third centuries there were Christians who believed that Jesus was both divine and human, God and man. There were other Christians that argued that he was completely divine and not human at all. (For them, divinity and humanity were incommensurate entities: God can no more be a man than a man can be a rock.) There were others who insisted that Jesus was a full flesh-and- blood human, adopted by God to be his son but not himself divine. There were yet other Christians who claimed that Jesus Christ was two things: a full flesh-and-blood human, Jesus, and a fully divine Christ, who temporarily inhabited Jesus' body during his ministry and left him prior to his death, inspiring his teachings and miracles but avoiding the suffering in its aftermath."

Finally, there were Christians who believed that Jesus' death brought about the salvation of the world. Others believed that

Jesus' death had nothing to do with the salvation of the world. There were other Christians who said that Jesus never died.

At the time the New Testament was written, the Gospels (written anonymously and later assigned the names of Matthew, Mark, Luke, and John) were made a part of it. Other Gospel books (discussed later in this Blog) were becoming available as sacred texts, read and revered by different Christian groups throughout the world.

But all these other Gospels, Acts, Epistles, and Apocalypses were viewed as heresy by the orthodox religious authorities of the day. As rich and as popular as these books were among early Christians, they were excluded from becoming part of the sacred scriptures or canon of Christianity. What eventually became the 27 books of the New Testament is only a subset of all

Christian literature that was once available to all Christians.

At the root of the development of orthodox views only of Christianity–was *politics*, even in the ancient world. Holding a conservative orthodox view of Christianity today is, as it was in early Christianity, to see only one view of Christianity. Just because it's a politically derived set of canonized scriptures doesn't make it any more descriptive of the historical Jesus than if those who were branded the heretics of Christianity instead had succeeded in dominating the sacred texts of Christianity.

Modern Day Differences of Opinion

Despite the orthodoxy of winning the battle to control the scriptures of early Christianity, large differences today exist among the world religions and the many denominations within Christianity itself.

Any particular church's doctrine may be at great variance, not only with other world religions and other denominations within Christianity, but with the very tomb of religious cannon itself that they promote as their source of authority–the Bible. There is wide variation of opinion regarding Christian doctrine espoused by skeptics, the general public, evangelicals, born-again Christians, notional Christians, agnostics and atheists, including differences by age, gender, and race.

Differences of opinion are the rule, not the exception, where the Bible is concerned. One group that has received a lot of media attention is known as the *Jesus Seminar.* This is a group of academic scholars who question the truth behind the Jesus of history and the Jesus of faith.

According to Lee Strobel, "The Jesus of history and the Jesus of faith: the Jesus Seminar believes there's a big gulf between the two. In its view the historical Jesus was a bright, witty, countercultural man who never claimed to be the Son of God, while the Jesus of faith is a cluster of feel-good ideas that help people live right but are ultimately based on wishful thinking."

One of the great apologists for Christianity was C.S. Lewis (1898-1963). Many younger generations may more likely remember C.S. Lewis for his creative fictional work, "The Lion, The Witch, and the Wardrobe." C. S. Lewis was one of the great defenders of the Faith since his conversion to Christianity in 1931. There were many Christians at Oxford in the

1940s. Many, like Lewis, felt that both the *pros* and *cons* of the Christian religion should be discussed openly. This led to the foundation of the Socratic Club. C.S. Lewis served as its president until 1954 when he became a Professor of Medieval and Renaissance English Literature at Cambridge University, England.

Many scholars today probably would dismiss Lewis' logic as nothing more than Socratic debate double-talk, or that his underlying assumptions about the relationship of natural to supernatural things or events made no sense at all. There was one statement in the Preface to Lewis' book that did make a lot of sense. That is, Walter Hooper wrote, in the preface to Lewis' book, *God in the Dock*, "Regardless of one's education, it is impossible to decide whether Christianity is true or false if you do not know what it is about." The methodology, of course, of knowing what something is about, should be based on observation, knowledge, and interpretation of the facts and assumptions made.

Interpretation of the Bible itself is made further difficult by the conflicts between various texts. There are texts within the New Testament that conflict with one another as well as conflict with those sacred texts that were rejected by the Orthodox Church. These rejected texts may have been more representative of who Jesus was and what Christianity was about than those texts that eventually became the "Orthodox view" of the Bible people read today.

For example Elaine Pagels reports in, *Beyond Belief–The Secret Gospel of Thomas*, "Christian mystics, like their Jewish and Muslim counterparts, have always been careful not to identify themselves with God. But the gospel of Thomas teaches that recognizing one's affinity with God is the key to the kingdom of God." Pagels goes on to say that, "Orthodox Jews and Christians, of course, have never wholly denied affinity between God and us. But their leaders have tended to discourage or, at least, to circumscribe the process through which people may seek God on their own. This may be why some people raised as Christians and Jews today are looking elsewhere to supplement what they have not found in Western tradition."

Where Does the Old Testament Come From?

It is important for people to understand that "the stories of the Bible evolved slowly over centuries before the existence of orthodox religions. Many belief cults spread stories and myths handed down by oral tradition from generation to generation long before people wrote them down. Many of the stories originally came from Egyptian and Sumerian cults.

All of these early religions practiced polytheism, including the early Hebrews. Some of the oldest records of the stories that later entered the Old Testament came from thousands of small cylinder seals depicting creation stories, excavated from the Mesopotamia period. These early artifacts and artworks (dated as early as 2500 B.C. E.) established the basis for the Garden of Eden stories at least a thousand years before it impacted Hebrew mythology."

How eventually were these stories written? It depended upon different languages. According to Martin Manser, "The two main original languages of the Bible were Hebrew and Greek. The Old Testament was mostly written in Aramaic. The entire New Testament was written in

Greek, the language commonly spoken and written throughout the Roman Empire in the 1st and 2nd centuries A.D."

Today original writings of the Old Testament do not exist. What does exist are hundreds of fragments from copies that became the Old Testament. The original material of the Old Testament was handed down as mythological stories via oral tradition. When scribes got into the act of writing the Old Testament they began to use Cuneiform tablets, papyrus paper, leather etchings and the famous Dead Sea Scrolls.

The writers or scribes of the Old Testament, as mentioned wrote in classical Hebrew except for some portions written in Aramaic. "The traditional Hebrew scribes wrote the texts with consonants but the Rabbis later added vowels for verbal pronouncing…In the second century C.E., or even earlier, the Rabbis compiled a text from the manuscripts as had survived the destruction of Jerusalem in 70 C.E...This text incorporated the mistakes of generations of copyists, and in spite of the care bestowed on it, many errors of later copyists also found their way into it. The earliest surviving manuscripts of this text date from the ninth to eleventh centuries C.E. It comes mostly from these texts which religionists have used for the present Old Testament translations."

Where Does the New Testament Come From?

In a nutshell, "Scholars have long debated whether Matthew, Mark, Luke, or John actually penned the Gospels. Because John and Matthew were thought to be original disciples and Mark and Luke were companions of Paul, their names may have been used to add credibility to the account.

Many scholars argue that the gospel writers were disciples of disciples or members of communities who were influenced by Paul or the disciples."

Pastor William R. Grimbol regards the Gospel writers as editors. According to Grimbol, "Although the primary sources for the story of Jesus are the Gospels, the Gospels are not firsthand accounts. The writers of these books were not reporters. The Gospels were recorded several decades after the events of the life of Christ. They were written from the perspective of looking back upon Christ's life and forward in anticipation of his return. The Gospels were not your average history books. The gospel writers gathered many patches of oral tradition concerning the life of Jesus. Each gospel writer received several of the same patches, some that were slightly different, and a few that were unique. Each gospel writer then weaved these patches together with the thread of his personal faith standpoint."

There is great discontinuity in the bibles that were created. First, the material of the Bible came from many unknown authors spread over a great expanse of time. One thousand two hundred fifty years separates the beginning of the writings on the Old Testament to the end of such writings (1450 B.C.E. to 200 B.C.E.).

It is believed that any New Testament writings didn't begin to be written until more than 30 to 95 years after the death of Christ. It is believed that Christ died in 30 C.E. "The Gospels cannot really be dated, nor are the real authors known. It is based on speculation that Mark was the first, written between 60 and 70 A.D., Matthew second, between 70 and 80 A.D., Luke (and Acts) third, between 80 and 90 A.D., and John last, between 90 and 100 A.D." The Epistles were written by the Apostle Paul long before the first Gospels were created. These Epistles were written between 48 and 58 C.E.

"All of the Gospels except John contain possible allusions to the destruction of Jerusalem, which was destroyed in 70 C.E., and thus it is likely they were all written after that date." Also, there appears nothing in Paul's letters that either hints at the existence of the Gospels or even of a need for such memoirs of Jesus Christ.

Some scholars believe that in 90 C.E. Old Testament books called, "The Writings," were created as part of the Christian Canon. The Writings included Psalms, Proverbs, Job, Song of Songs, Ruth, Lamentations, Ecclesiastes, Esther, Daniel, Ezra, and Chronicles.

It is also reported that, "The oldest copy of the New Testament yet found consists of a tiny fragment from the Gospel of John. Scholars dated the little flakes of papyrus from the period style of its handwriting to around the first half of the 2nd Century C.E. The language of most of the New Testament consists of old Greek." In 150 C.E. two important events occurred: (1) the four Gospels were collected and put together, and (2) The School of Alexandria was founded in Egypt, quickly becoming a major center for both Christian Theology and Greek Philosophy.

What many Christians fail to understand is that, in addition to the four Gospels of the New Testament, there were many other texts created by the early Christian religion. But these texts were suppressed [These texts will be discussed in detail in the next section]. They were known as the Agnostic texts, and were very important to early Christianity.

The first recorded use of the term "Christian" occurred at Antioch, Syria, home of one of the first Christian Churches.

The backdrop of the path of how today's Bible became what it is, is based on modifications over the last 2000 years. According to the history of the Dark Bible, "There has existed over a hundred different versions of the Bible, written in most of the languages of the time including Greek, Hebrew, Aramaic, and Latin. Some versions left out certain biblical stories and others added stories.

The completed versions of the Old and New Testaments probably got finished at around 200-300 C.E. although many disputed the authenticity of some books which later ended up as Apocrypha (un-canonical or of questionable authorship). For example, the book of Ecclesiastics appears in the Catholic Bible but not in Protestant versions."

A Bogus Christianity Based on an Incomplete Bible

On December 25th, 2005, and later during the spring of 2006, the History Channel presented an outstanding 2-hour world premiere documentary called, "Banned from the Bible." The reader must understand that many Christian documents and gospels on Christ and Christianity may have been destroyed or lost during the last 2000 years. However, many gospels and related documents were not lost or destroyed. They were simply banned from the Bible. What makes the extant Bible the **Word of God**? Why wouldn't the volumes of excluded documents also be the **Word of God**? And if so, who appointed whom to be the editor of God's word? Could it be then that the existing bogus Bible really had nothing to do with giving voice to God's word if men decided what was and was not the **Word of God**?

It is obvious to religious scholars that these books were in some way objectionable and threatening to the leaders of the orthodox Christian churches. Anything that did not meet with their approval was branded as *heresy*. Many of the books that were available as possible candidates for inclusion in the New Testament were, in fact, very popular with early Christians.

Like today early Christians hungered for any information about Christ. The extant Bible today is a *bogus* version representing the life of Christ in only an incomplete and limited way. Other Christian beliefs, such as those of the Agnostics never saw the light of day, even though many might argue better represented the true nature of Jesus Christ and Christianity. Interpretation and the derivation of meaning from any scriptures are patently unintelligible if the original sources of literary importance were excluded.

"One hundred and fifty years after the birth of Jesus, a man named Marcion decided that a Christian Bible was needed to replace the Hebrew Bible. Church leaders opposed Marcion's banning of the Hebrew books, but they did agree that Christians should have a Bible of their own.

After Constantine the Great converted to Christianity in the 4th century, a serious effort was made to compile a Christian Bible, one that included both the Hebrew Scriptures (the Old Testament) and Christian manuscripts (the New Testament). It took another 40 years before a final list of New Testament books was officially canonized by the church. Many of the most popular were excluded. Upon examination today, many of these writings attempt to resolve inconsistencies and questions raised from reading the bible."

As pointed out, more gospels and documents were left out than were included. To say that the Bible is the word of God is to miss the mark in a big way. The Bible was the political creation of conservative, Orthodox Church leaders in the 4th century that determined what was included, and what wasn't included in the Bible.

It is interesting to note in Bart D. Ehrman's book, *Lost Christianities* when he points out, "It is striking that, for centuries, virtually everyone who studied the history of early Christianity simply accepted the version of the early conflicts written by the orthodox victors. This all began to change in a significant way in the nineteenth century as some scholars began to question the 'objectivity' of such early Christian writers as the fourth-century orthodox author Eusebius, the so-called Father of Church History, who reproduced for us the earliest account of the conflict. This initial query into Eusebius's accuracy eventually became, in some circles, a virtual onslaught on his character, as twentieth-century scholars began to subject his work to an ideological critique that exposed his biases and their role in his presentation. The reevaluation of Eusebius was prompted, in part, by the discovery of additional ancient books, uncovered by trained archaeologists looking for them and by Bedouin, who came across them by chance, other gospels, for examples, that also claimed to be written in the names of apostles."

Banned Sacred Texts

A short synopsis of some of the banned sacred texts follows. Each of the books was *excluded* from the canons of Christianity:

- *The Life of Adam and Eve:* A more detailed story of creation than what is found in Genesis, this book includes jealous angels, a more devious serpent, and more information about Eve's fall from grace from her point of view.
- *The Book of Jubilees*: This obscure Hebrew text offers an answer to a question that has vexed Christians for centuries – if Adam and Eve only had sons and if no other humans existed, who gave birth to humanity? This text reveals that Adam and Eve had nine children and that Cain's younger sister Awan became his wife. The idea that

humanity was born of incest would have been radical – and heretical.

- *The Book of Enoch:* This scripture reads like a modern day action film, telling of fallen angels, bloodthirsty giants, an earth that had become home to an increasingly flawed humanity and a divine judgment to be rendered. Though denied a place in most Western Bibles it has been used for centuries by Ethiopian Christians. Large portions of this book were found as part of the Dead Sea Scrolls.
- *The Infancy Gospel of Thomas:* The only book that deals with young Jesus, it indicates that Jesus was a strong-willed child who one historian describes as "Dennis the Menace as God." The book reveals that at age five, Jesus may have killed a boy by pushing him off a roof and then resurrected him. Perhaps too disturbing for inclusion in the Bible, this book seems to contain traditions, also known to the Koran.
- *The Protovangelion of James:* This book offers details of the life of the

Virgin Mary, her parents, her birth and her youth; stories not found in the New Testament Gospels but was beloved by many early Christians.

- *The Gospel of Mary:* This Agnostic Text reveals that Mary Magdalene may have been an apostle, perhaps even a leading apostle, not a prostitute. While some texts in the Bible seem to deny women a voice in the Christian community, this text helps spark the debate about the role of women in the church.
- *The Gospel of Nicodemus:* This is the story of Jesus' trial and execution and descent into hell. According to this gospel, the Savior asserts his power over Satan by freeing patriarchs such as Adam, Isaiah and Abraham from Hell.
- *The Apocalypse of Peter:* Peter's apocalypse suggests that there is a way out of punishment for evildoers and implies that the threat of the apocalypse is a way for God to scare people into living a moral life, and committing fewer sins.

"These books are just a sampling of the hundreds that were never included in the Holy Bible. Perhaps there are more to be found. Whether one believes these alternative stories or not, they do provide an interesting perspective of the religious culture and propensities of the time."

On April 7, 2006 a bombshell rocked the world of modern day Christianity. Another book that had never made its way into the "official Bible" was discovered and found to be, through carbon dating, authentic. After 1700 years The Gospel of Judas was rediscovered. "Judas Iscariot, long reviled as history's quintessential betrayer, was actually the best friend of Jesus and turned him over to authorities only because Jesus asked him to, according to the Gospel of Judas." The long-lost document was revealed by the National Geographic

Society. The document is considered by some to be the most important archaeological find in the last 60 years. It "purports to record conversations between Jesus and Judas in the last week of their lives—conversations in which Jesus shared religious secrets not known by the other disciples."

This particular gospel, like many others above, was ruled heretical by early church leaders because of its disagreement with the conventionally accepted Gospels of Matthew, Mark, Luke, and John. According to Thomas H. Maugh II, writer for the Los Angeles Times, "Biblical scholars, however, hailed the new text because of the insight it will provide into the exceptionally turbulent period when competing ideologies sought to stake their own claims to the Jesus story, battling in oral stories and written texts until a single, faction eventually won out."

This writer's article, which appeared in the Sacramento Bee, also reported that, "Scholars said the 26-page document was written on 13 sheets of papyrus leaf in ancient Egyptian, or Coptic, and was bound as a book, known as a codex. It is one of dozens of sacred texts from the Christian Gnostics, who believed that salvation came through secret knowledge conveyed by Jesus."

The Great Problem of Biblical Interpretation

One of the greatest problems for Christian believers and non-believers alike is interpretation of biblical scriptures. Historically, this is shown and demonstrated by the plethora of major denominations and splinter groups in the Protestant movement alone. Different groups reflect different perspectives on Christian practice, theology, and the underlying meaning of scripture. All of this is aside from the many religions worldwide that have very different systems of belief from Christianity.

Fundamentalists in Christianity are more likely to believe in a 'literal' interpretation of the Bible. What exactly is a literal interpretation?

According to Donald K. Campbell, "when we interpret the Bible literally we interpret its words and sentences in their natural, normal, and usual sense." He quotes Merrill F. Unger as saying the literal method is "the method which seeks to arrive at the precise meaning of the language of each of the Bible writers as is required by the laws of grammar and the facts of history." At the heart of this approach is to derive 'meaning' from the scriptures.

The literal method does not preclude figures of speech such as symbols, allegories, metaphors, and similes.[1] The literal method recognizes that sometimes poetical and allegorical language is used to support a literal meaning of the Bible. Natural meaning, rather than literal words, per se, is secondary to natural meaning that provides context to underlying biblical truth.

Campbell further asserts that the more important principles of literal interpretation of the Bible include: (1) grammatical interpretation, (2) contextual interpretation, and (3) passages in the Bible have one meaning that should be determined prior to any moral application of the passage.

However, A.R. Bernard, Pastor of the Christian Cultural Center in Brooklyn New York, says "interpretation of the bible is more than literal." That is, he describes the interpretation of the Bible as literal, figurative, and symbolic.[1] According to Campbell and Bell, coming to agreement about what the Bible means has been quite a difficult task.[1] Both authors attribute difficulty to three factors: (1) a changing culture, (2) different and changing religions, and (3) different ways of understanding sacred writing. Within the Christian faith alone there is a plethora of opinions on what scriptures mean.

Whether something is told as a parable or that appears to be hyperbole, the words themselves always need to have their meaning deciphered. Campbell and Bell generally agreed (also an opinion) that the Bible provides God's truth for our lives, but how to interpret that truth is another matter.

These authors also say, "One reason you need to check out the bible on your own, rather than limiting your knowledge to what we tell you, is that people vary in their opinion of what is to be taken literally and what is figurative or symbolic."

According to Christian scriptures, only God possesses absolute truth, not man. However, it is still man who must interpret scriptures. If this were not so there wouldn't be so many religions and so many different denominations within Christianity itself. "We all tend to draw those lines in different places, and it's no simple matter to say that one person is right and another wrong."[1] How right one is ought to follow some degree of *logic* and *reason*, two things fundamentalists reject, ironically, even when defending their own positions.

Unfortunately, there are extremes in how scripture is interpreted. Some splinter Christian groups use snakes in their services, and others employ mentally unbalanced oppressive interpretations of God and scripture. Such was the case with charismatic leaders David Koresh of the Branch Dravidians, and Jim Jones of Jonestown.

Freedom of religion is a key freedom in every democracy; but to be really free democracy requires that there also be freedom *from* religion. Problems of interpreting the morality underlying many stories in the Bible are very significant. Seeing the Bible as a source for moral conduct is not only problematic, but downright immoral.

Using the Bible as any source for moral conduct is not only highly misplaced judgment, but highly dangerous in its implications. Problems of moral interpretation of the Bible reach far beyond the difficulties individuals have with ordinary contradictions and nonsensical or bizarre statements found in the Bible. There are more moral contradictions in the Bible than there are speeders on the nation's freeways. Rather than address all of them I will concentrate on just a few.

Is God A Loving God or a Murderous Thug? You Decide.

In the Bible, many people, including children, are slaughtered. Does God want children to die as some sort of whim? In Matt 18:14. It reads, "It is not the will of your Father which is in heaven, that one of these little ones should perish." One might conclude from this passage that God doesn't want any children to die. However, he often kills children and commands others to do so as well. In Gen.7: 21-22. God drowns all children (except for Noah's) in a worldwide flood. In Gen.19:24. God kills all of the children of Sodom and Gomorrah, and in Gen. 22:2. God tells Abraham to kill his son for a burnt offering. Gee, what a loving God!

One must remember that fundamentalists believe in a "literal" interpretation of the Bible. If one does take a literal view, as fundamentalists tell us we should when reading and interpreting the Bible, one certainly can't simultaneously take a symbolic or metaphorical interpretation just to be able to deny the acts of violence and mass murder committed by a monotheistic God. Fundamentalists must also accept these acts of murder as the will of God.

In Exodus 21:15; Lev. 20:9 and Deut.21: 18-21. The word of God says, "Children who are disobedient, or who curse or strike their parents are to be killed. In 1 Samuel 15: 2-3. God orders Saul to kill all of the Amalekite children, and in 2 Samuel 12: 15, 18, and 20, to punish David for having Uriah killed, God kills David's newborn son. In Deut. 20:16. and Joshua 10:40. God orders the Israelites to kill everyone including the children in the cities that they invaded.

Another area of interest is modern day Christian writers. One of the most influential contemporary religious writers is Lee Strobel. Lee Strobel has written several books on Christianity including *The Case for Faith, The Case for Christ*, and *The Case for the Creator.* In the *Case for Faith,* as in his other books, he takes the approach of stating objections to Christianity as a kind of intellectually presented "straw man."

His Objection # 4 (in *The Case for Faith*) is "God Isn't Worthy of Worship If He Kills Innocent Children."[1] Next in the process he conducts interviews of key religious scholars or academic theologians for their answers.

On the surface this appears to be straightforward and objective. One of his interviews was with a religious expert, Norman L. Geisler. In one example, God orders genocide by telling the Israelites in Deuteronomy 7 to totally destroy the Canaanites and six other nations and to show them no mercy. "God orders the execution of every Egyptian firstborn; He flooded the world and killed untold thousands of people; He told the Israelites to now go attack the Amalekites and totally destroy everything that belongs to them. Do not spare them; put to death men and women, children, and infants, cattle and sheep, camels and donkeys."

Strobel asked a question, "How can people be expected to worship Him if he orders innocent children to be slaughtered? Geisler's answer was some odd statement about how evil the Amalekites had been, and God's motive for committing murder. Strobel again asks the question by pressing him, "Why Did Innocent children need to be killed?" Geisler's answer then took off in the direction of the totally bizarre. He said "that technically nobody is truly innocent because we're all born in sin." Here the Christian concept of Original Sin is invoked again.

This ascribed status for all human beings (rather than judgment based on earned status) of being born in sin is presumably one of God's justifications for murdering children. Classifying children as full of sin is similar to what often happens to victims of violent crime in the criminal justice system in modern day society. *That is, the victim is blamed for the acts of the criminal.* For example, "She had it coming to her. She got raped because she lured me." Blaming the victim is to misplace responsibility for the acts of the offender. When children are blamed through some religiously simplistic explanation of original sin, it only reinforces the non-believers perception that people within Christianity are at best, misguided, or at worst, really stupid.

The Key to Salvation: Faith or Good Works?

One of the key doctrines of Christianity is salvation. Some believers of the faith believe salvation is by faith alone. What the Bible says is pure unadulterated contradiction. In Mark16:16. "He that believeth and is baptized shall be saved; but he that believeth not shall be damned."

It is said in Acts 16:30-31., "Sirs what must I do to be saved?" And they said, "Believe on the Lord Jesus Christ, and you will be saved–you and your household."[1] However, in Psalm 62:12. "For you render to each according to his works," and in Jer.17: 10. "I the Lord…give every man according to his ways, and according to the fruits of his doing,"[1] and in Matt. 16: 27. "For the Son of Man will come in his glory of His Father with His angels, and then he will reward each according to his works."[1] And in addition there is James 2:17. "Thus also faith by itself, if it does not have works, it is dead."

Contradictions in scripture are one reason why we have some Christian denominations telling their members that salvation is based on faith alone, while other denominations are preaching salvation by works alone, and others may be saying you can't have one without the other. This emphasis on salvation, either way or both, probably varies from church to church.

An Approach to Overcoming Conflict with Biblical Interpretation

One of the directions in the twenty-first century is toward theistic evolution. This is an effort on the part of some scientists and theologians to bridge the gap between science and religion. Despite the long standing conflict between the two approaches to knowledge and the seeking of "Truth," there may be a middle ground. Not everyone agrees that there can be a middle ground.

If religion, and in particular Christianity, wants to extricate itself from its losing position in the world today, it will have to take a more reasoned approach (albeit scientific methodology) and play by a different set of rules. In all likelihood this repositioning of the rules of the game will be easier for mainline Protestant groups, already many of whom have no quarrel with science or scientists.

Theologians and fundamentalists who pay lip service to wanting to bridge the gap need to remember the words of Clint Eastwood to Liam Neeson in *The Dead Pool*, "If you want to play in the game love, you better know what the rules are."

That means take nothing in religion on faith. Test everything according to the rules of scientific inquiry. In other words prove whatever claims are made. Let the chips fall where they may. Let there be no straw men in such testing, but rather the testing of genuine real hypotheses about biblical scripture.

Even if science isn't brought to bear in the field of religion and theology, it is very likely that conservative fundamentalists, evangelicals, and others who demand a literal translation of biblical scriptures, will continue to experience a losing uphill battle. This is their propensity to view religious dogma in "absolute" terms. This entrenched position, of course, not only flies in the face of, not just scientific knowledge that contradicts scripture, but competition from other major religions and challenges from other denominations within Christianity itself.

In addition, there is absolute widespread ignorance among most Christian church-goers in the United States on the very history of Christianity itself. There is a need to improve the education of Christians themselves. Instead of teaching Christianity from a doctrinal point of view (and doctrine is the "psycho-babble of religion"), church-goers would be better off initially if they endeavored to learn the actual history of their own religion. Because of this need, education needs to be more detailed as to all of the decision-making points in Christianity.

How the Bible was put together in the first place, and how theological issues were decided at various points in Christian history had a tremendous bearing on what finally came forward from the 4th century on as to the "accepted" content of the Bible Christians use today. Much needs to be learned about 4th Century activities that changed Christianity.

Many questions need to be evaluated and discussed. Why did early Christians high-jack the Torah, the first five books of the Bible from Judaism? Where did the idea of the Trinity come from (Father, Son, and Holy Ghost)? What was the conflict of Christ's status as either man or God, or both, and why wasn't it officially decided until 325 C.E?

While answers to these questions are available in the academic literature on Christianity, very few church-goers have an interest in developing a deeper understanding of the very religion they lay claim to believe in. Some believers want to maintain a comfort zone of belief independent of any effort to learn the facts of the very religion they believe in. The notion of justification of beliefs and faith was covered in my book, Trouble in Paradise: The Decline of Christianity in the 21st Century. The specific chapter was Chapter XI , *Religious Beliefs versus Rationality*.

Despite the sometimes antagonistic relationship between science and religion, it must be remembered that some scientists, namely biblical archaeologists, have contributed a great deal toward our understanding of the ancient world of the Middle East. Biblical Archaeology, however, has never been able to affirm the divinity of Christ, his miracles, or even his character. What it has been able to do is connect many of the locations and identify (through artifacts) many of the events, individuals and empires described in the Bible.

Psychology

Chapter 10

The Mind/Brain or Mind/Body Dichotomy in Psychology

Introduction

The purpose of this chapter is to review one of the longest standing issues in psychology--- known as the mind/brain or mind/body dichotomy. It is a critical long-standing issue in psychology because various assumptions about the mind/brain connection affect so many different sub-fields within psychology. In turn, it's important to be up front about this issue because of its significance in developing any kind of theory in psychology today.

The Mind/Brain Dichotomy

The following is an article by Saul McLeod published in 2007.

"The **mind** is about mental processes, thought and consciousness. The **body** is about the physical aspects of the brain-neurons and how the brain is structured. The mind-body problem is about how these two interact.

One of the central questions in psychology (and philosophy) concerns the mind/body problem: is the mind part of the body, or the body part of the mind? If they are distinct, then how do they interact? And which of the two is in charge?

Many theories have been put forward to explain the relationship between what we call your mind (defined as the conscious thinking 'you' which experiences your thoughts) and your brain (i.e. part of your body).

However, the most common explanation concerns the question of whether the mind and body are separate or the same thing.

Dualism vs Monism

Human beings are material objects. We have weight, solidity and consist of a variety of solids, liquids and gases. However, unlike other material objects (e.g. rocks) humans also have the ability to form judgments and reason their existence. In short we have 'minds'.

Typically, humans are characterized as having both a mind and body. This is known as **dualism**. Dualism is the view that the mind and body both exist.

There are two basic types of dualism:

> o **Descartes dualism**: The view that the mind and body function separately, without interchange.

> o **Cartesian dualism** argues that there is a two-way interaction between mental and physical substances.

Dualism is in contrast to Monism that states the mind and body is the same thing.

There are two basic types of Monism:

o **Materialism** is the belief that nothing exists apart from the material world (i.e. physical matter like the brain); materialist psychologists generally agree that consciousness (the mind) is the function of the brain. Mental processes can be identified with purely physical processes in the central nervous system, and that human beings are just complicated physiological organisms, no more than that.

o **Phenomenalism** (also called **Subjective Idealism**) believes that physical objects and events are reducible to mental objects, properties, events. Ultimately, only mental objects (i.e. the mind) exist. Bishop Berkeley claimed that what we think of as our body is merely the perception of mind. Before you reject this too rapidly consider the results of a recent study.

Scientists asked three hemiplegic (i.e. loss of movement from one side of the body) stroke victims with damage to the right hemispheres of their brains about their abilities to move their arms. All three claimed, despite evidence to the contrary in the mirror in front of them, that they could move their right and left hands equally well. Further, two of the three stroke victims claimed that an experimental stooge who faked paralysis (i.e. lack of movement) of his left arm was able to move his arm satisfactorily.

Psychology & the Mind Body Debate

There are different approaches to psychology contrasting views as to whether the mind and body are separate or related. Thinking (having freedom of choice) is a mental event, yet can cause behavior to occur (muscles move in response to a thought). Thinking can therefore be said to make things happen, 'mind moves matter'.

Behaviorists believe that psychology should only be concerned with "observable actions," namely stimulus and response. They believe that thought processes such as the mind cannot be studied scientifically and objectively and should therefore be ignored. Radical behaviorists believe that the mind does not even exist.

The biologists who argue that the mind does not exist because there is no physical structure called the mind also follow this approach. **Biologists** argue that the brain will ultimately be found to be the mind. The brain with its structures, cells and neural connections will, with scientific research, eventually identify the mind.

Since both **behaviorists and biologists** believe that only one type of reality exists, those that we can see, feel and touch; their approach is known as Monism. Monism is the belief that ultimately the mind and the brain are the same thing. The behaviorist and biological approaches believe in materialism monism.

However biologists and behaviorists cannot account for the *phenomenon hypnosis*. Hilgard and Orne have studied this. They placed participants in a hypnotic trance and through unconscious hypnotic suggestion told the participants they would be touched with a "red hot" piece of metal when they were actually touched with a pencil.

The participants in a deep trance had a skin reaction (water blisters) just as if they had been touched with burning metal. This is an example of the mind controlling the body's reaction. Similar results have been found on patients given hypnosis to control pain. This contradicts the monism approach, as the body should not react to unconscious suggestions in this way. This study supports the idea of dualism, the view that the mind and body function separately.

In the same way **humanists** like Carl Rogers would also dispute materialism monism. Humanists believe that subjective experiences are the only way to study human behavior. Humanists are not denying the real world exists, rather they believe it is each person's unique subjective approach to defining reality that is important. In the area of mental illness a Schizophrenic might not define their actions as ill, rather they would believe they had insight into some occurrence that no one else had. This is why humanists believe the study of how each person views themselves is essential.

However, the problem of the relationship between consciousness and reality from a subjective view has problems. The paranoid schizophrenic who believes the postal service "are agents for the government and trying to kill him" is still mentally ill and needs treatment if they are not to be a danger to themselves or the public.

Recent research from **cognitive psychologists** has placed a new emphasis on this debate. They have taken the computer analogy of Artificial Intelligence and applied it to this debate. They argue that the brain can be compared to computer hardware that is "wired" or connected to the human body.

The mind is therefore like software, allowing a variety of different software programs to run. This can account for the different reactions people have to the same stimulus. This idea ties in with cognitive mediational (thinking) processes. In computer analogies we have a new version of dualism which allows us to incorporate modern terms such as computers and software instead of Descartes 'I think therefore I am.'"

The following was also written by Saul McLeod in 2007.

"The term cognitive psychology came into use with the publication of the book *Cognitive Psychology* by Ulric Neisser in 1967.

Cognitive Psychology revolves around the notion that if we want to know what makes people tick then we need to understand the internal processes of their mind.

Cognition literally means "knowing." In other words, psychologists from this approach study cognition which is 'the mental act or process by which knowledge is acquired.'

Cognitive psychology focuses on the way humans process information, looking at how we treat information that comes in to the person (what behaviorists would call stimuli), and how this treatment leads to responses. In other words, they are interested in the variables that mediate between stimulus/input and response/output. Cognitive psychologists study internal processes including perception, attention, language, memory and thinking."

My Evaluation of the Mind/Brain Dichotomy

My own personal take on the Mind/Brain or Mind/Body dichotomy goes something like this: You destroy the body with its brain, and the mind goes away too. However, the concept of a subjective reality that can be studied separately as a social construct is correct.

This debate over the mind/brain has created a kind of "false dichotomy." That is, it occurs to me that aspects of Dualism and Monism may be both right and wrong.

Descartes's Dualism is not correct because the mind and brain do interact. However, **Cartesian dualism is more precise.** It argues that there is a two-way interaction between mental and physical substances. I interpret this to mean that neurons and special parts of the physical brain communicate with one another. I do not interpret this to mean a separate mind/body dichotomy by introducing the term, "interaction."

The problem of dualism is that it fails to see the mind as an invented useful social construct for understanding and describing human behavior. The mind is not a separate physical entity.

Monism, however, is correct for promoting the general idea that the brain and the mind are one and the same. Carl Rogers, although disputing material Monism, was correct in pointing out the subjective reality of the mind and that subjective insights can be studied in their own right.

Just consider Harry Stack Sullivan's Interpersonal Theory of Psychiatry, Carl

Rogers own Client Centered Therapy, or the brilliant concepts of Sigmund Freud. All of these psychiatrists/psychologists built careers on the basis of the highly subjective nature of mental processes such as thoughts, feelings, and subjective perceptions. Using a social construct, these scientists were simply studying how the mind works within the brain.

One needs to stand back and marvel at how the human brain works. Unlike a robot, the mind has such incredible capability to set the conditions for "freewill," free thought and determination all within the fantastic realm of consciousness (and perhaps the subconscious and unconscious as well). It will take time, however, before scientists can grasp all the intricacies of the interactions of the various parts of the brain. The prefrontal cortex and prefrontal lobes are intimately involved in decision-making once all information sources within the brain create the need for mind-generated action in the external world.

Freud however didn't necessarily concern himself with activities of the prefrontal cortex or lobes, or the belief that the unconscious mind might be located in a primitive brain stem. He didn't have too. The subjective realm of human behavior and what causes it was all he needed where his powers of observation were concerned.

Just as Freud invented his own unique social constructs (Ego, Id, Super-ego), he readily made use (whether he realized it or not) of the social construct nature of the "mind." What I'm saying is, the mind is not some metaphysical reality that somehow transcends the physical brain. We simply don't yet know enough to actually explain all "brain activity."

I think the mind concept, rather than a separate entity within the brain, is really a primarily individualized social construct that should be useful to scientific inquiry. What is a construct? A construct in psychology is basically "a social mechanism, phenomenon, or category created and developed by society; a perception of an individual, group, or idea that is 'constructed' through culture or social practice." Likewise, the concept of mind is very much a social construct. Here is a definition of mind: "the element of a person that enables him/her to be aware of the world and their experiences, to think and to feel; the faculty of consciousness and thought."

As a social construct, the mind relates to the concept of a subjective reality. This viewpoint is also nonetheless correct. That is, every mental thought, image, perception, sensation, beliefs or values, are important variables influencing human behavior.

Our consciousness allows all sorts of sensory input, as it relates to both objective reality and subjective interpretation of those sensations or perceptions. The internal interactive nature of thoughts, sensations, perceptions all interact and relate to memory, language, awareness and thinking. Computer circuitry operates at an exceptionally high speed; but it pales by comparison to the human brain that operates at "warp speed."

Chapter 11

A New Social Psychology Theory of Human Need Fulfillment

"Immature love says: 'I love you because I need you.' Mature love says 'I need you because I love you.'"
— Erich Fromm

Purpose of Blog

The purpose of this chapter is to set the stage for a new theory of human need fulfillment in social psychology. It will be known as "*A New Social Psychology Theory of Human Need Fulfillment.*" One of the important existing theories in psychology that deals with human needs is Abraham Maslow's Hierarchy of Human Needs.

I find the motivational theory of Abraham Maslow relevant in modern society and, therefore, generally reasonable. Human needs were articulated and well-described by Maslow many decades ago. The needs Maslow discussed come down to survival, basic and social needs.

However, it is important now to move ahead and articulate what it takes to fulfill a person's needs. Basically, the question is what factors or variables are responsible in an individual that creates the conditions whereby one's needs are met?

How does one even begin to approach thinking about how needs are satisfied? Theoretically this is a huge undertaking. In this author's opinion there are five macro level social domains or categories that might capture the variables involved in human need acquisition. These five categories include:

Broad-Based Social/Structural Forces

These are societal broad-based sociological forces such as: economy, national, state and local laws and policies, and war.

Categorical Characteristics of the Individual

These are variables like age, race, and gender, level of education, income level, being married, divorced or single, current social class, and social class and marital status of one's parents.

Intra Psychic/Psychiatric Characteristics of the Individual

These are variables like self-esteem, self-image, interpersonal relationships, one's outlook on life, capacity to love, extent of feelings of confidence and/or competence, level of emotional stability and mental maturity.

Fortuitous Events

These are variables like accidents and unexpected life changes like sudden disability, losing a job, or unusual events like winning the lottery or death/disability of a family member.

Inherited Characteristics of Individuals

These are variables like intelligence, special talents, body type, blood type, birth weight and any disabilities or diseases at birth.

Proposed Research Question

I propose this primary question for study: **What variables (among the five macro level social domains or categories) best explain human need fulfillment.** Although Abraham Maslow told us what our needs are, both independent and dependent variables need further explanation. What explains the degree of success in meeting one's needs during a lifetime? What makes all this incredibly complex is that an individual's needs can change over time. For example, certain needs may need to be "put on hold" if one is going through a rough patch in life.

Prior Research and Assumptions

Looking at the five domains of variables I am going to suggest theoretically that not all domains are likely to predict or explain success in meeting one's needs. I preliminarily hypothesize that human need fulfillment is best explained in terms of Carl Rogers concept, a fully functioning person. This leads one to ask what a fully functioning person is.

What is a Fully Functioning Person?

According to Carl Rogers, a fully functioning person is one who is in touch with his or her deepest and innermost feelings and desires. These individuals understand their own emotions and place a deep trust in their own instincts and urges. Unconditional positive regard plays an essential role in becoming a fully functioning person.

Rogers suggested that people have an actualizing tendency, or a need to achieve their full potential – a concept that is often referred to as self-actualization. Rogers believed that a fully-functioning person is an individual who is continually working toward becoming self-actualized. This individual has received unconditional positive regard from others, does not place conditions on his or her own worth, is capable of expressing feelings, and is fully open to life's many experiences.

Defining the Fully Functioning Person

"Essentially, the fully functioning person is completely congruent and integrated. Such a person, Rogers believes, is able to embrace 'existential living.' By this he means they are able to live fully in the here and now with personal inner freedom, with all its accompanying exciting, creative, but also challenging, aspects."
(Freeth, 2007)

"Such a person experiences in the present, with immediacy. He is able to live in his feelings and reactions of the moment. He is not bound by the structure of his past learnings, but these are a present resource for him insofar as they relate to the experience of the moment. He lives freely, subjectively, in an existential confrontation

of this moment in life."
(Rogers, 1962)

"The fully functioning person has a flexible, constantly evolving self-concept. She is realistic, open to new experiences, and capable of changing in response to new experiences. Rather than defending against or distorting her own thoughts or feelings, the person experiences congruence: Her sense of self is consistent with her emotions and experiences. The actualizing tendency is fully operational in her, and she makes conscious choices that move her in the direction of greater growth and fulfillment of potential."
(Hockenbury & Hockenbury, 2006)

The Characteristics of a Fully Functioning Person

Characteristics of a fully functioning person include:

- Openness to experience
- Lack of defensiveness
- The ability to interpret experiences accurately

- A flexible self-concept and the ability to change through experience
- The ability to trust one's experiences and form values based on those experiences
- Unconditional self-regard
- Does not feel the need to distort or deny experiences
- Open to feedback and willing to make realistic changes
- Lives in harmony with other people

Rogers also developed a form of therapy known as client-centered therapy. In this approach, the therapist's goal is to offer unconditional positive regard to the client. The goal is that the individual will be able to grow emotionally and psychologically and eventually become a fully-functioning person.

The primary question posed in this Blog is related to Maslow's work. That is, if one can't fulfill needs he/she is unlikely to become a fully functioning person. Accordingly, if one becomes a fully functioning person, it increases the probability one is likely to fulfill their needs. Yet, there is always the possibility that a fully functioning person might not meet all their needs, while some individuals, not yet a fully functioning person, may nonetheless meet all their needs (perhaps fortuitous events intervene in a person's life).

Said another way, I believe there is an interrelationship between striving toward becoming a fully functioning person, and meeting one's needs in life. But what can clarify this interrelationship between need fulfillment and the fully functioning person is a research study. Until then it is theory in need of empirical evidence.

One day in the future it may be possible for an individual to keep score as to how well they are progressing toward becoming a fully functioning person. Before one gets to the pragmatic implications of a new theory---the theory of human need fulfillment of Abraham Maslow must first be articulated.

Human Need Fulfillment

Human need fulfillment is the process of satisfying one's basic and social needs. This goal of fulfilling needs is a lifetime endeavor for all of us, and can be thought of as a constant approach/avoidance conflict. **Approach-avoidance conflicts** as elements of stress were first introduced by psychologist Kurt Lewin, one of the founders of modern social psychology. It's important to note early that during one's lifetime there are many variables or factors that contribute or detract (obstacles) from meeting one's social, physical or safety needs.

But first, describing a new theory will need to be done in stages. There are certain areas of knowledge about psychology one needs to be aware of before one can fully understand a new theory within the context of social psychology.

Preliminary Contextual Framework

What is an Approach Avoidance Conflict?

"Approach-avoidance conflicts occur when there is one goal or event that has both positive and negative effects or characteristics that make the goal appealing and unappealing simultaneously.

For example, the popular culture construction of marriage is a momentous decision/goal/event that has both positive and negative aspects. The positive aspects, or approach portion, of marriage are togetherness, sharing memories, and companionship; however, there are negative aspects, or avoidance portions, including money issues, arguments, and mortgages.

The negative effects influence the decision maker to avoid the goal or event, while the positive effects influence the decision maker to want to approach or proceed with the goal or event. The influence of the negative and positive aspects creates a conflict because the decision maker either has to proceed with the goal or event or not partake in the goal or event at all.

To continue with the example of marriage, a person might approach proposing to a partner with excitement because of the positive aspects of marriage: having a lifelong companion, sharing financial responsibilities. On the other hand, he or she might avoid proposing due to the negative aspects of marriage: arguments, money issues, joint decision making.

The approach side of this type of conflict is easy to start toward the goal, but as the goal is approached the negative factors increase in strength which causes indecision. If there are competing feelings to a goal, the stronger of the two will triumph. For instance, if a woman was thinking of starting a business she would be faced with positive and negative aspects. Before actually starting the business, the woman would be excited about the prospects of success for the new business and she would encounter (approach) the positive aspects first: she would attract investors, create interest in her upcoming ideas and it would be a new challenge.

However, as she drew closer to actually launching the business, the negative aspects would become more apparent; the woman would acknowledge that it would require much effort, time, and energy from other aspects of her life. The increase in strength of these negative aspects (avoidance) would cause her to avoid the conflict or goal of starting the new business, which might result in indecision.

Research pertaining to approach and avoidance conflicts has been extended into implicit motives, both abstract and social in nature."

It should be added that the approach/avoidance conflict may not be consciously recognized by many people. People often set unrealistic goals only to discover later the negative sides of goal acquisition. The more equipped people are in meeting their goals, the more likely they will succeed. The best way to be equipped, so a person can meet their needs, is to be or become---*A Fully Functioning Person.*

I'd like to point out before describing my testable hypotheses that scientists need to further refine any testable hypotheses with *operational definitions* for terms such as self-actualization, self-esteem, self-image, mental maturity, ego-ideal, interpersonal relationships, beliefs, values, achievement, etc. Also, readers need to understand the basics of this scientific process. Here is a definition of variables and their needed operational definitions:

Variables are anything that might impact the outcome of your study or can take on different values (primarily numbers or categorical values as well.) An **operational definition** describes exactly what the variables are and how they are measured within the context of one's study. For example, if you were doing a study on the impact of sleep deprivation on driving performance, you would need to operationally define what you mean by *sleep deprivation* and *driving performance.*

In this example you might define sleep deprivation as getting less than seven hours of sleep at night, and define driving performance as how well a participant does on a driving test.

What is the purpose of operationally defining variables? The main purpose is control. By understanding what you are measuring, you can control for it by holding the variable constant between all of the groups or manipulating it as an independent variable. I want to point out that operationally defining the outcome (dependent variable) will not only be important but a great challenge as well.

Sigmund Freud presented to the world some amazing concepts based on the cornerstone of all science, observation. But Sigmund Freud did not carry out any kind of systematic social research using statistics and statistical analysis. What I'm proposing in the way of testable hypotheses are ideas to be tested in future social research. The ideas themselves are the easy part. Creating operational definitions for variables and carrying out the proper statistical analysis may be the hard part.

Introduction

Everyday observation suggests that some individuals are very successful in meeting their needs, while others seem like they just can't catch a break no matter what they do. The purpose of developing a new social psychology theory of human need fulfillment is to: **(1) improve upon Abraham Maslow's Theory, A Hierarchy of Needs, (2) explain the variables or factors that either lead to human need fulfillment, or cause needs not to be fulfilled, and (3) suggest two types of research studies in which questions proposed might be answered.**

Background for a New Theory in Psychology

One of the most important theorists on human needs was **Abraham Maslow** whose theory, **A Hierarchy of Needs**, became widely accepted both inside and outside the field of psychology. Before describing the set of facts that pertain to this theory, it is necessary to provide the reader with background on what theory is and what makes a good theory.

What is a theory?

A theory is much more than a guess or a hunch. A theory both describes a phenomenon and should make statements of prediction about future behaviors. The term *theory* is used with surprising frequency in everyday language. It is often used to mean a guess, hunch or supposition. You may even hear people dismiss certain information because it is "only a theory." It is important to note as one studies psychology and other scientific topics, that a theory in science is not the same as the colloquial use of the term.

A scientific theory is based upon a hypothesis and backed by evidence. A theory presents a concept or idea that is testable. In science a theory is a reasoned explanation for some phenomenon. In the simplest terms: **A theory is a fact-based framework for describing a phenomenon. In psychology, theories are used to**

provide a model for understanding human thoughts, emotions and behaviors.

A good psychological theory has two key components: (1) it must describe a phenomenon, and (2) it must make predictions about future behaviors. Ahead I will present Maslow's Hierarchy of Needs Theory, provide a critique of Maslow's Theory, then produce a set of theoretical propositions regarding the questions I earlier proposed.

Early Origin of an Idea

When I was a freshman in high school I read books on psychology in my spare time. One of the psychology books had a section on Abraham Maslow, a famous psychologist. He hypothesized a pyramid of human needs. The hierarchy of human needs model suggests that human needs must be fulfilled one level at a time.

According to Maslow's theory, when having fulfilled all the needs in the hierarchy, a human being may eventually achieve self-actualization. Late in life,

Maslow came to conclude that self-actualization (to be explained below) was not an automatic outcome of satisfying the other human needs.

Human needs as identified by Maslow:

- At the bottom of the hierarchy are the "Basic needs or Physiological needs" of a human being: food, water, sleep and sex.
- The next level is "Safety Needs: Security, Order, and Stability". These two steps are important to the physical survival of the person. Once individuals have basic nutrition, shelter and safety, they attempt to accomplish more.
- The third level of need is "Love and Belonging", which are psychological needs; when individuals have taken care of themselves physically, they are ready to share themselves with others, such as with family and friends.
- The fourth level is achieved when individuals feel comfortable with what they have accomplished. This is the

"Esteem" level, the need to be competent and recognized, such as through status and level of success.

- Then there is the "Cognitive" level, where individuals intellectually stimulate themselves and explore.
- After that is the "Aesthetic" level, which is the need for harmony, order and beauty.
- At the top of the pyramid, "Need for Self-actualization" occurs when individuals reach a state of harmony and understanding because they are engaged in achieving their full potential. Once a person has reached the self-actualization state, they focus on themselves and try to build their own image. They may look at this in terms of feelings such as self-confidence or by accomplishing a set goal.

Maslow's ideas have been criticized for their lack of scientific rigor. He was criticized by American Empiricists as scientifically too soft. In 2006, conservative social critic Christina Hoff Summers and practicing psychiatrist Sally Satel asserted that, due to lack of empirical support, Maslow's ideas have fallen out of fashion and are "no longer taken seriously in the world of academic psychology." Positive psychology takes a different view. Positive psychology spends much of its research looking for how things go right rather than the more pessimistic viewpoint, how things go wrong.

Furthermore, the Hierarchy of Needs has been accused of having a cultural bias— mainly reflecting Western values and ideologies. From the perspective of many cultural psychologists, this concept is relative to each culture and society and cannot be universally applied. Maslow's concept of self-actualizing people was later united with Piaget's developmental theory.

While some research showed some support for Maslow's theories, most research has not been able to substantiate the idea of a needs hierarchy. Wahba and Bridwell reported that there was little evidence for Maslow's ranking of these needs and even less evidence that these needs are in a hierarchical order.

Other criticisms of Maslow's theory note that his definition of self-actualization is difficult to test scientifically. His research on self-actualization was also based on a very limited sample of individuals such as Albert Einstein and Eleanor Roosevelt.

Regardless of these criticisms, Maslow's hierarchy of needs represents part of an important shift in psychology. Rather than focusing on abnormal behavior and development, Maslow's humanistic psychology was focused on the development of healthy individuals.

While there was relatively little research supporting the theory, hierarchy of needs is well-known and popular both in and out of psychology. In a study published in 2011, researchers from the University of Illinois set out to put the hierarchy to the test. What they discovered is that while fulfillment of the needs was strongly correlated with happiness, people from cultures all over the world reported that self-actualization and social needs were important even when many of the most basic needs were unfulfilled.

Observations

For two and one half years I've been playing international chess against players all over the world. We all strive for excellence in playing chess. Few of us will ever achieve the pinnacle of perfection. Only a handful out of the 7.5 million players on the web will ever be another Bobby Fischer or a Magnus Carlson in today's chess world. Trust me. Maslow's Hierarchy of Needs applies to most everyone in affluent, industrialized nations, regardless of their general culture.

Nevertheless, with chess players there is a "selection bias" when trying to generalize. Many populations in the world spend their entire lives just trying to secure their safety and basic needs for food, water, sleep and sex. There are always individual exceptions when it comes to striving for higher levels of human need, but the reality is a high percentage of people in many countries live below the poverty line. Their basic modus operandi is plain and simple---survival and the acquisition of basic human needs. However, as the 2011 study from the University of Illinois suggested, social needs and self-actualization were considered important even when many of the most basic needs were not (just consider the starving artists of the 1930s).

A Critique---Abraham Maslow's Hierarchy of Needs

In general I think Maslow's Hierarchy of Needs, despite some possible cultural bias, is a *reasonable theory* of human motivation. The one major criticism I do have of Maslow's theory is that, in terms of absolute priority or need levels described in his theory, I think our **safety/survival** needs most often take precedence over the basic needs of food, water, sleep, and sex. Also, at any point in time safety/survival needs may take precedence over all higher level needs as well. Example: You may be polishing up a paper that will award you the next Nobel Prize in Particle Physics. But if your house is suddenly consumed in fire the safety/survival need kicks in and you flee from your house. Your self-actualizing moment of writing a paper worthy of the Nobel Prize will have to wait.

Nevertheless, there are exceptions. We are all constantly trying to satisfy our needs or the needs of those we love. In fact, higher level needs (particularly love, belonging, self-image and self-esteem) may override one's need to survive or risk one's safety in deference to saving loved ones over one's own survival.

Terrible threats directed at oneself or family members often cause individuals to take flight or to fight and perhaps risk great harm. Most people tend to take flight (example---people running away from a shooter in a mall or on a college campus). Yet, some individuals would rather fight by disarming or killing the assailant. Said another way---a social need may take priority over one's personal safety. That social need might best be described as a kind of **social survival where values and beliefs play an important role.**

Another example is this. Everyone wants to survive, but during military combat operations, frequently, individuals will protect or defend their buddies even when such actions may put them in harm's way.

In other words, even the survival need is socially evaluated and determined, i.e., survival does not always control human actions. And one's intrinsic values may influence behavior more than mere survival. What values you ask? How about values such as honor, duty, country or protecting one's immediate family and loved ones from harm?

Now, the psychological need for self-actualization is very compelling in otherwise superior individuals. However, for some individuals, achievements, or self-actualization, may not be important at all. Rather, some people would prefer to acquire or achieve status, position, or wealth than to engage unnecessarily, or strive for, self-improvement or acquire skills to realize one's own full potential.

Our basic "fight or flight mechanisms" generally overrule all other human considerations most of the time. It gets very complex even here when social needs (see above) come into play. Meeting human needs is not orderly or hierarchical in real life; human behavior is much more complex. Everyday life and the meeting of our needs at all levels are always momentarily "conditional."

Our brain is constantly organizing, re-organizing and prioritizing our physical and social needs and their conditional nature at every moment (conditional in the sense of making choices and evaluating one's physical and social needs).

Understanding how the brain operates in this need striving/conditional environment requires a social construct known as the "mind." For this author there is no mind/brain dichotomy. The mind (complex parts of the brain and neural structures) and the body are physically the same. However, as social scientists, we make use of a social construct in order to understand the complex workings of the brain. As said above, that social construct is called the "mind."

While the brain is constantly mediating priorities in fulfilling our needs, one might legitimately ask, from a scientific perspective, what really underlies all such brain-activated mediation?

In statistics, a **mediation** model is one that seeks to identify and explicate the mechanism or process that underlies an observed relationship between an independent variable and a dependent variable via the inclusion of an explanatory variable (s), known as a mediator variable(s). This explanatory variable or variables is crucial to all decision-making.

There are two aspects to a mediator variable(s): (1) the process of evaluation itself (conditions, evaluation, what-if questions) and (2) the additional sensory input used to make a decision. In other words, variables or factors in a mediation model dictate our behavioral choices at any point in time.

This gets very complicated (when one is talking about thinking) because the mediating process itself of evaluation is always influenced by our feelings and emotions. A cognitively rational decision isn't always the decision people make. The brain may decide, following all sensory input, (despite looking at conditional aspects, evaluation, or internally answering what-if questions) that the best decision isn't necessarily a rational one. We are not machines. We are endowed with all sorts of sensory input including psychological variables like feelings, perceptions and emotions.

Rather than hypothesizing a direct causal relationship between the independent variable and the dependent variable, a mediational model hypothesizes that the independent variable influences the mediator variable(s), which in turn influences the dependent variable.

Thus, the mediator variable(s) serves to clarify the nature of the relationship between the independent and dependent variables. Once again, mediating relationships occur when a third variable or set of variables plays an important role in governing the relationship between the two other variables. I want something (a personal decision to fulfill a need). The "wanting" serves the role of the independent variable. The dependent variable is the result (actually meeting or satisfying the need).

The brain however says, "Wait a minute." The brain then initiates or introduces the mediating process variable(s) (evaluation, conditions, and what-if questions). In addition, other sensory or perceptual variables may come into this process. These may be variables like self-esteem, self-confidence, self-image, feelings, values and/or beliefs to name a few.

Overview of Theory

I am proposing a new theory of human need fulfillment predicated on knowing what variables predict human need fulfillment. First and foremost, *fulfilling any need does not occur in a social vacuum.* Therefore, I predict the domain known as **[Intra Psychic/Psychiatric Characteristics of the Individual]** will better predict human need fulfillment than any other domain. The variables I believe that best determine whether one's needs are met are: self-esteem, self-image, interpersonal relationships, one's outlook on life, capacity to love, feelings of confidence or not, extent of competence (social or intellectual), emotional stability, and mental maturity.

The concept of a fully functioning person was first articulated by Carl Rogers (1966). All striving after human need fulfillment (this author's opinion) is based on an Approach/Avoidance Conflict. Values, beliefs, psychological make-up, and prior social learning cause one to strive to meet human needs (whether they are survival/safety, basic or higher level needs).

The Five domains and their variables can be used to answer the primary hypothesis mentioned earlier. Initially, there may be hundreds of variables that have some predictive power in correlating with a well-defined output variable, such as need fulfillment. There may be stages of life related to age that may differ as to outcome since people usually move forward as they age. Needs differ at each stage of life, because individuals may simply redefine what their needs are.

Given the importance of developing a better explanation of what causes our needs to be fulfilled, it is crucial to determine what variables are most highly correlated with the dependent variable (human need fulfillment).

Once the data are available, one of the early steps in a research study will be to generate a correlation matrix. This must occur prior to any attempt to reduce the number of predictive variables to the parsimonious few. This is the point at which factor analysis and other multivariate approaches become very useful to this type of analysis of variable reduction.

In terms of the parsimonious few, who knows, perhaps employment status, good health, strong interpersonal relationships and support systems (friends, significant others) , and self-esteem will best predict the outcome variable. But this is only an assumption, and it could be wrong. This is why research is the most exciting detective work of all. As Tom Hanks said in the movie, *Forrest Gump*, "You never know what you're going to get."

As said earlier, a good psychological theory has two key components: (1) it must describe a phenomenon and (2) it must make predictions about future behaviors. By prediction I mean there must be testable hypotheses.

It is my evaluation, based on prior research, that the most predictive variables (to be determined through factor and multivariate analysis) will turn out to be, at an individual level---*self-esteem, self-image, interpersonal relationships, one's outlook on life, capacity to love, feelings of confidence or not, extent of competence (social or intellectual), emotional stability, and mental maturity.*

These are the variables that really matter when it comes to fulfilling one's needs and whether one becomes a fully functioning person or not.

Testable Hypotheses

- The greater the amount of self-esteem one has, the greater their needs will be met

- The better a person's self-image, the greater their needs will be met

- The greater one's interpersonal relationships are, the greater their needs will be met

- The more positive a person's outlook on life, the greater their needs will be met

- The greater one's capacity for love, the greater their needs will be met

- The better one has feelings of confidence/competence, the greater their needs will be met

- The greater one is emotionally stable, the greater their needs will be met

- The more mentally mature one is, the greater their needs will be met

All that I've suggested up to this point is to initiate a preliminary set of steps toward developing a new theory in social psychology. I alluded to the possibility that some day it may be possible for someone to walk into a psychologist or school counselor's office, sit down and take a battery of tests that will not only tell a person where they are in life, but be given a detailed plan as to how to get back on track (i.e., what an individual needs to do).

But, before we get to that pragmatic stage of psychological services (no person left behind) much research needs to be done on need fulfillment.

There are many ways to research or answer the questions posed in this Blog. I will write, in the future, more topics in the field on psychology (the fears in our lives, the Mind/Body or, etc.). In the meantime, I have some suggestions as to how a new theory in psychology needs to be researched.

How best to test this theory scientifically

There are two special ways to test hypotheses in research: (1) sampling and taking measurements at one point in time, and (2) conducting research with a longitudinal cohort study. Both approaches have research value.

The value of the first approach is obtaining early clues on prediction of the outcome variable(s). The value of a longitudinal cohort study is understanding variables and their interactions over time i.e., as things change. **My preference is to conduct both types of studies.** With the longitudinal approach two studies come to mind: **The Farmington Heart Study** and another longitudinal study known as *Delinquency in a Birth Cohort* developed by the famous sociologist Marvin Wolfgang.

The Farmington Heart Study of Cardiovascular Disease has been going on for 65 years. In 1948, the Framingham Heart Study embarked on an ambitious project in health research to identify the common factors that contribute to cardiovascular disease by following its development over a long period of time among a large group of participants.

The study conducted by Wolfgang, Figlio and Sellin was known as "Delinquency in a Birth Cohort." It was conducted in Philadelphia, Pennsylvania between 1945 and 1963. The purpose of this study was to investigate the history of delinquency in a birth cohort--in particular, the age of onset of delinquent behavior and the progression or cessation of delinquency. Data were collected on a cohort of males born in 1945 and residing in Philadelphia, Pennsylvania. Information provided in the study included demographic characteristics of the individuals studied, academic performance, offense information, demographic characteristics of victims, and criminal incident information.

For any researchers out there who think studying how a person becomes fully functioning would be worthwhile, the data collection aspect of a study demands operationally well-defined input and output variables, perseverance and proper funding. As social scientists we have many clues, mostly socio-demographic, psychological and psychiatric, that can identify why people fail during their lives, or are unable to lead fruitful lives. Like Abraham Maslow we need to look at the positive side of the ledger, i.e., why people succeed.

Imagine what findings from this type of study might do to assist politicians, and give them direction as to how best to help their fellow citizens achieve their goals and objectives in life. What better role might a politician play than meeting, or helping to meet, the needs of their constituents?

In the spirit of positive psychology and Abraham Maslow, it's time to create a new chapter on why people succeed or fail in life. But also it is very important to discover why many individuals who experience great difficulties in life, nevertheless are tenacious enough to succeed anyway. Such a study, looking at three sides of a coin (top, bottom, and its edge) might generate incredibly important information for society.

About the Author

Dr. Roy V. Lewis is a U.S. Navy combat veteran during the Vietnam War, and a retired administrator from the California Department of Justice.

Prior to retirement, he worked 32 years as a criminal justice administrator and criminologist researcher. He worked primarily for the California Youth Authority and the California Department of Justice. While working for the California Department of Justice, Dr. Lewis managed the Statistical Data Center (SDC), largest depository of criminal justice data and information in the United States at the state level.

During his career Dr. Lewis published multiple research journal articles, government studies, program evaluations, and reports on various criminal justice topics. In 1969-70 Dr. Lewis studied for a (J.D.) degree at the University of the Pacific McGeorge School of Law. Dr. Lewis has a

Bachelor of Arts (B.A.) in Psychology from San Francisco State University, a Master's degree in Public Administration (M.P.A.) with Phi Kappa Phi honors from the University of Southern California, and a Doctor of Philosophy (Ph.D.) degree from Columbia Pacific University.

Dr. Lewis is active in many organizations including the National Senior Games Association (NSGA) and United States of America Track and Field (USATF). He was an active participant in the 2011 World Masters Athletics Championship games as a member of *Team USA*. In his age group at the time he came in 6th in the world in the javelin throw, 12th in the weight throw, and 17th in the shot put. In 1994 Dr. Lewis achieved the golfer's dream---he scored a hole-in-one at Rolling Greens Golf Course near Granite Bay, California; he also has a 14 handicap.

In his spare time, he enjoys oil painting, theatre arts, coaching/mentoring, writing, and world chess competition. Dr. Lewis is also a member of Amnesty International, The Bright's, and d-Life Foundation.

Dr. Lewis has written 13 books (ten nonfiction books and three novels). His non-fiction books include: *Juvenile Diversion* (Oelgeschaler, Gunn and Hain, 1980) which he co-authored with another researcher and scholar (Dr. Ted Palmer); *White Collar Crime and Offenders–A 20-Year Longitudinal Cohort Study* (Writer's Club Press, 2002); *The Reasoned Society (Rational Critique on Issues of the Day) Series I* (Lulu, 2009); *Trouble in Paradise--- The Decline of Christianity in the 21st Century* (Surge Publishers, 2009); *The Reasoned Society (Rational Critique on Issues of the Day) Series* II (Lulu, 2010); *Insight: Sociology and Critique of Today's Cultural Issues* (Create Space Publishers, 2013); and Insight: Critical Social Issues of Our Time (Create Space Publishers, 2013); Insight: Important Sociological Issues in the 21st Century (Create Space Publishers,

2015); Sociology of Today's Critical Social Issues (Create Space Publishers, 2015) and Lurking in the Shadows (Create Space Publishers, 2015).

Dr. Lewis has also published three novels; *American Hawk* (iUniverse.com, 2003); *Night of the Cougar* (VBW Publishing, 2007); and *Jackals' Lair* (Create Space Publishers, 2010). He is currently working on his 14th book, an autobiography titled, *Growing Up in Marin County during the 1940s and 1950s*. All his current books are available on **Amazon.com**.

He was editor and publisher (1996-98) of *Twenty-First Century Crime and Criminal Justice–an international criminal justice newsletter*. His Blog, **The Reasoned Society**, has now acquired more than 37,000 views since its inception in May, 2008. It is published monthly on WordPress.com. He enjoys commenting on social issues and has published an editorial in the Sacramento Bee, Letters to the Editor, and an article (2009) in Sacramento News & Review.

Newspaper and magazine articles have been written about Dr. Roy V. Lewis including the **Folsom Telegraph** [Master's Track helps senior improve health], **Second Act** [5 Athletes Who Inspire This Summer], and **Sacramento Talent Magazine** (primarily about his background and oil paintings).

Dr. Lewis currently makes his home in northern California.